SYMBOLS
of My Father's Love

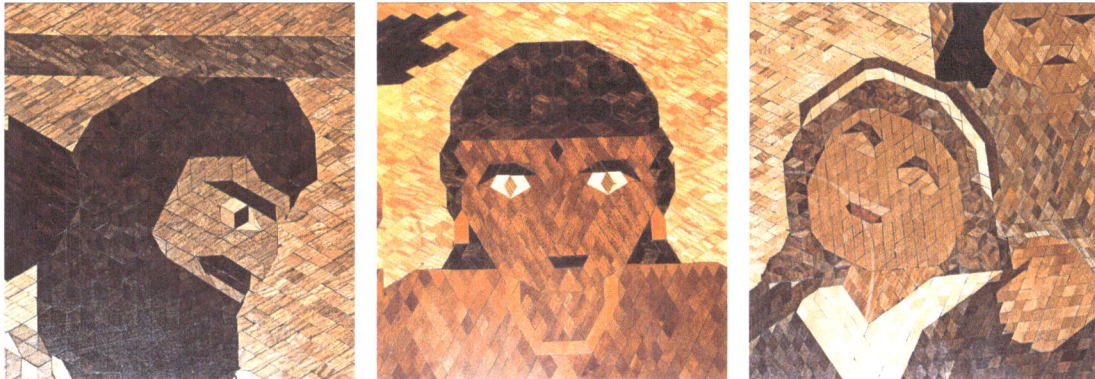

SYMBOLS
of My Father's Love

Concepts and interpretations
inspired by Ed Lantzer

JEANNINE TAYLOR

First Edition: November 2018

Cover Design: Jeannine Taylor

Cover Image: Donated by Friends of Foulds Gallery, Libertyville, Illinois

ISBN 978-0-578-41454-6

ACKNOWLEDGEMENTS

There are so many people I wish to acknowledge and thank for their roles in helping me write this book. Without their generosity, professionalism, resources, patience, and love, I could never have accomplished this momentous task.

John and Anita Wilson and their foundation, Pennies from Heaven, gave a sizable financial contribution to My Father's Love Foundation that made writing and publishing this book possible. My sincere gratitude to you both for your generous donation.

Daniel Harrigan, professional editor and proofreader (www.danielharrigan.net), agreed to proof and edit this book without even knowing me. He learned about the book from a board member of My Father's Love Foundation, and agreed to donate his time. Daniel, I am so thankful for your graciousness and your professional expertise.

Dale Hull, non-profit consultant and teacher at St. Michael Academy of Petoskey, also donated his time to proofread and edit this book. Dale was formerly a board member of My Father's Love Foundation, and knew Ed personally. Thank you so much, Dale, for taking the time to help me effectively tell this story.

Amber Brandt, freelance copywriter and editor, is a dear friend of mine and also donated her time to proofread this book. Amber was a part of my video production team and was by my side when we captured footage of Ed explaining the panels in the old Kalkaska warehouse. She was blessed to meet Ed and to contribute to his story in several ways. Thank you, Amber.

Chris Sundberg provided video footage of an interview he had with Ed when the panels were on display in Petoskey, Michigan. Thank you, Chris. Your video helped put the pieces together on Ed's meanings for the panels.

Friends of the Foulds Gallery in Libertyville, Illinois, for generously donating several photos used throughout this book. Thank you for bestowing your amazing talent and your beautiful photos of the panels.

LaShelle VanHouten, my amazing sister, for introducing me to Ed, and for believing in me and supporting me as I took on this project.

My Father's Love Foundation for entrusting me with this ever-important undertaking.

Trent, Logan, and Brock Taylor - the loves of my life - for your patience and your support.

TABLE OF CONTENTS

PREFACE

The journey to writing *Symbols of My Father's Love* was a lovely one. I'm blessed to be the sister of LaShelle VanHouten, the former school teacher whose class was selected to learn the art of marquetry from artist and recluse, Ed Lantzer. It was then that my sister's life changed forever, and so had mine.

LaShelle became Ed's confidant, his storyteller, and even somewhat his soul mate. She immediately recognized Ed was divinely placed in her life, and she knew she would be a significant part of his life until he died. While secretly living and working in an old warehouse to finish his life's work, Ed taught LaShelle and her students his craft and recounted to her his life story as she documented every word. She knew one day she would be the one to tell Ed's story to the world.

I came into the picture in 2005 as a resource for LaShelle while she worked to capture Ed's story. At the time, I owned a video production company, and after talking to LaShelle about her quest, I offered to bring my team in to shoot footage of Ed teaching her students how to do marquetry. I remember the day we arrived with our gear and laid eyes on the panels for the first time. I was overwhelmed by the sheer size and intricacy of the images before me. The details and symbolism were unlike anything I had ever seen.

We set up the camera and lights and began shooting as Ed explained the meaning behind each panel, and the symbols he'd delicately placed in each of them. At that moment, I understood the significance of what we were doing. We were gaining an education and acquiring knowledge from the artist himself on the enormous story he depicted in these panels; a story way beyond what is seen at first glance.

Fast forward four years and Ed Lantzer left this world to see his maker face to face. With him, he took his stories, his descriptions, and his love for all God's children. The meanings and symbolism Ed meticulously situated into each panel are mostly a mystery to those who view them.

LaShelle kept her promise to Ed and told his life story in her book, *The Mural Writer*. She also sits on the Board of Directors of My Father's Love Foundation (MFLF), started by Ed to care for and protect his panels, ensuring they are always free for all to see. When on display, members of MFLF and other volunteers act as docents who try to explain the special meanings of the panels and their unique symbols to awe-struck visitors. The foundation recognized the need for a reference book to delve deeper into the symbolism Ed deliberately included and to expound on what Ed referred to as his thought patterns as he created the panels. This was when I came back into the picture.

A marketing and communication professional by trade, I love the process of digging deep to find the nitty-gritty details to develop campaign ideas. In the back of my mind, I wanted to be the one to take on this project from the very start. Aware that MFLF was actively looking for someone to write the book, I approached them to throw my hat in the ring. After much consideration, I was selected for the project and got to work right away.

Is it divine intervention that the videos my company shot all those years ago ended up being a substantial tool in writing this book, and that I would be the one writing it? As Ed would say, "You decide." These videos, along with another series of videos shot by Chris Sundberg while Ed and the panels were in Petoskey, Michigan, provided first-hand information from Ed himself. Additionally, I spent many months scouring the Internet researching to find the meaning behind Ed's most elaborate concepts, ancient terminology, biblical references, and the multiple languages he utilized to create this masterpiece.

I feel extremely blessed to be a small part of such an enormous story. I am forever grateful to My Father's Love Foundation for their confidence in me and their patience as I worked to put together the pieces of this puzzle. I am also thankful for my sister LaShelle for her loving support and unending encouragement. She stayed close by to provide guidance when I needed it, but also remained at arm's length to let me do my thing.

My husband, Trent, and sons, Logan and Brock, are my world and gave me the space I needed to accomplish this mission. I so appreciate their understanding as my eyes were glued to the computer for days on end.

This book is meant to be a guide—answering the many questions about what the symbols in the panels mean—and what Ed's thoughts were as he embedded them into his designs. Each chapter displays one panel series with letters on the panel images that coincide with descriptions of each image. I enhanced several of the images within each panel by darkening or lightening them so they can be more easily seen. For ease of understanding, the chapters are not ordered chronologically by when Ed created each series, but as the stories were chronologically told in the Bible.

Throughout the book, I reference Ed's own explanations and words that came directly from his mouth as they were captured in the videos. I utilized research to corroborate his descriptions in an effort to validate his stories and his many years of studying ancient texts, languages, cultures, and religions.

I hope that those who read this book are enlightened by the enormity of Ed's work and walk away with a better sense of his love for the Father and for who he calls "the unloved child." It was important to Ed that all those who view the panels make their own decisions on the meanings of the symbols, wood choices, colors, and designs. When asked, Ed would do his best to explain his meanings, but would always finish with, "You decide."

- Jeannine Taylor

ED LANTZER, THE ARTIST

Ed was born in Kalkaska, Michigan in 1932, and led a tumultuous life. At age four, he contracted scarlet fever that damaged his brain, making it difficult for him to write or to draw. His baby brother also became ill and died, prompting Ed's mother to blame Ed for his brother's death. She was furious and told Ed he was incapable of loving. These words stayed with Ed for the rest of his life. He was socially awkward, often bullied, and never felt that he fit in anywhere.

Ed's father taught him the art of parquetry and marquetry, artforms used to decorate floors, furniture and artwork that require placing pieces of wood side by side to create patterns and shapes. The eighth generation of Lantzers to master the skill, Ed's father showed him how to make squares and cubes using very precise 90-degree and 45-degree angles to cut the wood. Eventually, Ed's father claimed that those precise angles were his signature angles and he told Ed to find his own angle. Ed decided the diamond shape (with 30-degree and 60-degree angles) was his preferred choice because with them he could make beautiful curves in wood. He practiced his skills by making game boards, chests, boxes and tables.

Ed married his high school sweetheart and they soon had their first child. Sadly, their baby daughter suffered complications and was stillborn. Her death sent both Ed and his wife into deep despair. Ed's mother's words came screaming back, "You are incapable of loving!" While he and his wife went on to have eight more children, their marriage was strained and Ed eventually left them, telling himself they were better off without him.

From then on, Ed worked odd jobs, got into trouble, spent time in the state mental institution, and was kicked out of the state of Michigan by a judge. He went to Florida where he was homeless and struggled to survive. Eventually he found work in the building trade and even worked for Walt Disney where he built cabinetry and shelving for some of the buildings in Disney World.

Eventually, Ed earned enough money to rent a small place with a tiny workshop where he could get back to practicing his artform, mar-

quetry. It was there that he had his first vision about creating a large piece of art. It was an image of the Last Supper made completely out of small diamond-shaped pieces of wood. At first, Ed was overwhelmed by the thought and convinced himself it was too hard. Besides, he couldn't write down his thoughts or even sketch any ideas. God, however, had different plans. It soon became clear to Ed that this was the job God chose for him and he would receive what he needed to get it done.

Ed studied the Bible, researched ancient religious texts, and read as many books as he could for inspiration; books like *Mere Christianity* by C.S. Lewis. Ed found wood wherever he could, searching through dumpsters and receiving donations from people who knew about his quest. He started cutting diamond shapes using his 30-degree and 60-degree angles, and soon his vision became clearer as he contemplated difficult formulas in his head. Finally, equipped with a 4-foot by 8-foot piece of plywood and some Elmer's Wood Glue, Ed attached the first piece of wood to the board. He intuitively placed it just below the chin in the throat area of what would eventually become the body of Jesus. Seven sheets of plywood, 8 feet tall, 28 linear feet, 2,800 pounds, and tens of thousands of diamond-shaped wood pieces later, Ed's first panel series was complete.

Ed displayed his artwork at a diner owned by people he'd befriended. It didn't take long, however, for him to start feeling very protective of the panels. Fearing that others may want to profit from them, Ed packed them up and left town without anyone knowing. Finding himself back in his hometown of Kalkaska, Ed was homeless once again. He eventually took refuge in an old schoolhouse where he worked on more panels. Forced to leave there, he moved into an old warehouse where he set up shop to work on the panels, and secretly lived there, with no running water and no toilet, for years. This is where Ed felt safe, away from those who wanted to take the panels he called his "children," his life's work, away from him.

Soon, everything would change. Ed met some people who had his best interest, and the interest of the panels, at heart. Ed formed a foundation to see to it that the panels would be cared for, protected, and never used for personal gain or profit. He called the foundation "My Father's Love" to symbolize the purpose for the panels—to show all children, especially those who feel unloved, that they are loved by our Father in heaven. Ed's primary requirement was that the panels be available, free of charge, for all to see. No individual, organization, or corporation can ever lay claim to them in order to make a profit.

After 24 years during which Ed created over 2 million individual, hand-cut, diamond-shaped pieces of wood, he finished his last panel. Ed lived long enough to see them displayed for thousands of people in Petoskey, Michigan and Evansville, Indiana. Ed died in 2009 at the age of 77.

To learn more about My Father's Love Foundation, visit www.myfatherslove.info. To learn more about Ed Lantzer, the artist, read *The Mural Writer* written by LaShelle VanHouten.

THE PANELS

AdamEve

Moses and the Ten Commandments

My Mother's Love

My Father's Love

Simon and the Lamb

Raising of Christ

The Best Man

Daddy

The Quest

The Veil

ADAMEVE

The story of Adam and Eve takes place in Genesis, the first book of the Bible. God created Adam, and then his companion, Eve, and placed them in the Garden of Eden to care for his creations. Ed constructed this panel to tell their story and explains that this is a story within a story, rich with symbols and special meanings.

A. In the center of the panel is a rectangle, which Ed calls the "walls of creation." It is God's temple, but it is continually under construction. Ed claims that there will never be an end to our discovery because all that is created is new and continues to develop. Creation is actually the melody of the universe, the most beautiful song of love the Great Energy sings as He creates. We are all the center of His creation, each with a job to do. Our first job is to love each other and ourselves. Another meaning Ed gives to the golden rectangle is that it represents the Holy Spirit, the female.

B. Inside the rectangle is a diamond, which Ed calls the "circle of God." It is shaped like a diamond because He is priceless. Ed also calls it the value of the temple, representing the Great Energy's mind and what He is thinking. His son, who was crucified to help us understand who we are, is always at the center of His mind.

C. Displayed in the center of the diamond is the letter T, which is a symbol of the cross called the Tau (pronounced Taw) Cross. The Tau Cross is also known as the Old Testament Cross because it was mentioned in Ezekiel 9:4 *"And the Lord said to him: Go through the midst of the city, through the midst of Jerusalem: and mark Tau upon the foreheads of the men that sigh, and mourn for all the abominations that are committed in the midst thereof."* It is also known as the "Anticipatory Cross" because it foreshadows the crucifixion.[1]

Ed also describes the T as his totem, like the Native Indian totem pole. Ed says his totem is a history of his precepts and his thinking from his studies and work. The panels are his totem because they tell his history. He says, "if we met on the street and someone says, 'What do you do,' I couldn't answer, 'I do nothing and yet I am busy all of the time, thinking, planning, building, adding to my totem.' It tells you what I believe, what I think, and what I think is sacred. We are on very sacred ground."

Another explanation Ed gives for the diamond and cross inside the box is that the box represents eternity, and many people feel they are boxed in with no way out; that they are trapped for this eternity. Ed says the solution is in the Tau, or the cross. The Tau is in the center of eternity, and everything is built on the cross—the good, the bad, the indifferent. If we show people the box and ask them to read about Adam and Eve, they will find their way out of the box themselves. We are not in a box, and if we feel that we are, then it is our own thinking that has boxed us in.

D. Below the rectangle is the Bible.

E. Under the Bible is the word "READ." Ed says

that by reading and studying the Bible, we can become free to be who we are meant to be.

F. Around the rectangle is a serpent eating its tail, which is the universal symbol for eternity, or death and rebirth. The name for it is "Ouroboric," a Greek word meaning "tail swallower." It appears in various cultures including Egyptian, Gnosticism, Alchemy, Norse, Aztec, and Chinese.[2]

Ed explains that the serpent eating its tail is also symbolic of the resurrection, life from death. Jesus died on the cross so that we could have eternal life.

G. Above the serpent is the "Sword of Truth," which the Father will use when eternity is finished to shut it all off and start over again. Ed explains that there is no actual ending, but the Great Energy will take a sword and stop this eternity. This place where we are now will be destroyed and will revert to its original self.

The sword is also thought to be the word of God, the "Sword of the Spirit." In Ephesians 6:17, Paul says, *"Take the helmet of salvation and the sword of the Spirit, which is the word of God."* This isn't the only place where God's word (the Bible) is described as a sword. The author of Hebrews also makes reference to it: *"For the word of God is living and powerful, and sharper than any two-edged sword, piercing even to the division of soul and spirit, and of joints and marrow, and is a discerner of the thoughts and intents of the heart. And there is no creature hidden from His sight, but all things are naked and open to the eyes of Him to whom we must give account"* (Hebrews 4:12-13).

Another meaning Ed gives for the sword is that it is symbolic of the story of King Arthur who pulled the sword from the stone because he was the only pure knight in Camelot. After his death, another knight picked up the sword, held it high in the air, and threw it to the Lady in the Lake who, upon catching it, sunk to the bottom of the lake because she

1 "Cross of Tau," Symbols.com, accessed March 31, 2017, http://www.symbols.com/symbol/cross-of-tau.

2 "Ouroboros: Symbolic representation of coming full circle (cycle)," Ouroboros - Crystalinks, accessed March 31, 2017, http://www.crystalinks.com/ouroboros.html.

was not pure. Only those without sin could handle the sword.[3]

H. The names Adam and Eve are displayed together as one word, ADAMEVE, which Ed designed this way to signify one atom split in two. *"But for Adam no suitable helper was found. So the LORD God caused the man to fall into a deep sleep; and while he was sleeping, he took one of the man's ribs and then closed up the place with flesh. Then the LORD God made a woman from the rib he had taken out of the man, and he brought her to the man. The man said, 'This is now bone of my bones and flesh of my flesh; she shall be called 'woman,' for she was taken out of man.' That is why a man leaves his father and mother and is united to his wife, and they become one flesh."* (Genesis 2:20-25)

I. Under ADAMEVE is the name RACHEL, which Ed placed there to represent the female concept and the female way of thinking. In the Old Testament (Genesis 29; 30; 31; 33:1, 2, 7; 35:16-26; 46:19, 22, 25; 48:7), Rachel was the second wife of Jacob and the one he truly loved. Her older sister Leah was Jacob's first wife, and she had many children with him while Rachel was barren. This anguished Rachel for many years until God finally remembered her and she was able to give birth to two sons, Joseph and Benjamin.[4] Ed explains that it is Rachel's "thought pattern" for children, her cries for children, that he is representing. When she was barren, she felt she could not do the job the Great Energy created her for. We are all children of the Great Energy, each with a job to do, but Ed wonders where God's children are today. Have we advanced? Have we regressed? Are we doing our jobs? These are questions each one of us needs to answer for ourselves. If we are bored working a senseless job, maybe we need to change our concept of what our job is in order to experience the happiness of being a part of this great universe. Ed says he hasn't even started in his education and understanding of who and what he is. He is a child of the Great Energy, both male and female, in the family of humans, all created in the likeness of the Great Energy. He says, no matter how far you go out into the eternities, you are going to be asking the same questions, who are God's children?

J. Next to Rachel is Ed's signature, 6-22-34. This series of numbers comes from Joshua, the sixth book of the Bible, the 22nd chapter and the 34th verse which reads: *"And the children of Reuben and the children of Gad called the altar Ed: for it shall be a witness between us that the LORD is God."* Because Ed is a witness for the Lord, he made this scripture his artistic signature.

Continuing the story of Adam and Eve, it is important to note that this is the last panel Ed created before he died. He based his designs on abstract theories and his viewpoint of the female perspective. It all started in the Garden of Eden, according to Ed, where the female was created as a helpmate for her other half, the first Adam.

K. At the bottom of the panel is Adam created from the dust of the earth.

L. Coming up from Adam's side is Eve reaching upward for her own spiritualism.

M. Eve is also reaching for the apples so that she can fulfill her obligation to help Adam in every way so he can reach his destiny. Ed explains that he is always hungry and he likes to eat, so when Eve sees the apples, they distract her as she reaches for her own potential. When Adam sees this, he declares that he understands the female and that she is not lesser or second in creation; she is the same as he but has a different purpose. Just as the female needs to help the male reach his destiny, he also needs to help her reach hers, which is spiritualism, learning love, faith, and hope, so that she can express these virtues to the male. You can see there are darker apples, low hanging fruit, that are easier to reach, and lighter apples that are higher and more difficult to reach because they are pure.

3 "The Lady of the Lake," Britannia.com, accessed October 18, 2017, http://www.britannia.com/history/biographies/nimue.html.

4 "Rachel: The Woman in Whom Romance and Tragedy Were Blended," All the Women of the Bible - Rachel, accessed September 04, 2017, https://www.Biblegateway.com/resources/all-women-Bible/Rachel.

N. On Eve's right hand is the head of a snake. Ed explains that the snake in the Garden of Eden was Eve's right hand as she reached for the apple, but it also came from Adam. Eve became distracted by the apples as she reached for her spiritualism because she knew Adam was hungry. Represented here is the abstract theory of positive and negative working together at the same time—for every positive thought, there is a negative thought; for every action, there is a reaction. Distraction is a negative feeling, and negativity came into the picture at that very point when Eve became distracted by the apples. Ed's explanation here is that the snake was inside Eve and Adam, as it is in each one of us. It is our own thought pattern, our own ability to think for ourselves and make our own choices. When we make mistakes, we often blame it on something or someone else. What Ed is trying to explain here is that there wasn't an actual serpent in the Garden of Eden, but Adam and Eve's own thoughts and choices that caused them to eat the forbidden fruit. We all have positive and negative within us. Ed explains that the negative may be telling us one thing, but through logic, reason, and law, we learn the negative is wrong.

Ed also explains you cannot explain love through simply *saying* love; there has to be an action, though action itself, or alone, is not love. He gives the example of the 50 years he spent researching, learning marquetry, studying the different woods, exploring various concepts, and the only thing he was trying to express was, "I love you." No matter your experiences, you are a part of creation, and you are creation's brother and sister. When you look at all of Ed's work, the joining of the woods and concepts, he wants you to understand that he loves you. The love is not in the panels; it is inside him. He did this work for no other reason. Ed says, "I love, and it is the only way that I have to love, but in itself, it is not love at all. That negative/positive is there exactly." Ed explains that in understanding the concept that all things come from within, you will see that it is in our nature to try and understand ourselves and to bring us closer together rather than push us apart.

Ed wants us to understand that, as we look at his life's work, we see the point of it is the same as what we have in our own lives: We want and need to love something, and therein is the Great Energy. Eve is coming to the point of understanding who she is and what she is. She is soft, and she is what Adam needs as a helpmate. Ed explains that, while animals were created as God's servants, He placed them here to help us. They have duplicate meanings and missions, such as bringing us happiness and accommodating us on some things we need. The Great Energy did not create them because He needed them, but they supply a need within the male/female. For example, fish are not here for fish; they are here to fish. They live in the water, consume other fish and everything else in the water, and if you remove them from water they die. No matter what, animals cannot violate the law for which they were created. Fish were made to be in the water, so you will never see a fish walk around on dry ground. Likewise, we are dependent on our helpmate who helps us to love Love itself, which is the Great Energy. We are in a circle of love, and it is very tight and very positive, yet the negative goes right around with us. When we do bad things or make mistakes, negativity wants us to believe that the Great Energy hates us and that He created us to hate, to punish, to trip and to fall. In actuality, He wants us to experience the consequences of our mistakes but also to understand that we are learning, not being punished. We may feel pain, but pain is what makes these experiences memorable so that we learn from them.

O. Behind Eve is what Ed calls the "complete diamond." If you look closely, you see that it is actually two triangles joined together to make a diamond. While the traditional symbol for male is the triangle and for female is the upside-down triangle, Ed displayed them here in reverse to help tell his version of the story.

P. The top triangle represents the female as Eve is reaching up for her spirituality. The triangle has three points representing the female characteristics of faith, hope, and love.

Q. The bottom triangle, or the upside-down triangle, represents man being made from the Earth. It has three points that Ed says represents man's characteristics of law, knowledge, and wisdom. When you join the triangles together you get another point, a complete diamond, which Ed says is the Messiah, the Savior, the expectation of something that unites them exactly.

When you add the two triangle points together, 3+3, you get 6, which is the number of mankind and their weakness of sin.[5] When you add the point of the complete diamond to it, you get the number 7 (3+3+1=7), which is the number of perfection, the resurrection, and spiritual completeness.[6] Ed says by joining all of these concepts together, you see that it is man and woman joined together by their love, but they make mistakes because they are human. When you add the Messiah to them, they are forgiven and made perfect through Christ.

R. On each side of the diamond are what Ed calls the two pillars which represent the upright law, or the law in wisdom. In the first temple built, there was a pillar on each side of the entry that held up the roof as individuals came to be set apart from normality in this holy place.

S. 6-22-34 is displayed again, which is Ed's artistic signature and comes from the 6th book of the Bible—Joshua, chapter 22, verse 34.

T. A final thought Ed had while designing this panel is centered around the boot, or foot of Adam that extends from his leg onto the bottom of the *AdamEve* panel. Ed explains that the time of the crucifixion is like a reboot in time. He uses the example of how an electrical storm wipes out everything on your computer and you must reboot it by putting

all new symbols and history back in it, which takes time. The same is true after the crucifixion—everything starts over again for a second time. We have changed our principles and concepts, so we have rebooted. Now, we are not after the boot itself, but the toe (or the Tau, the cross). The toe represents the cross and it is the kickoff, or the booting of time again.

An additional concept Ed has for this panel is one he says most theologians and scholars do not go far enough in their thinking to consider. Ed explains that this panel also displays the scenario leading to the crucifixion. He says the Great Energy puts His son in a deep sleep, as He did when He created Adam. From the side of His son, the Messiah, emerged the Christian church. As Eve is the helpmate for Adam, the church is the helpmate, the companion, the friend of Christ. The Christian church was formed from inside Jesus and then taken outside for others to see. The story of creation is where the first Adam was formed, and the story of the crucifixion is where the second Adam was created and died for us all. Both are a product of God's love.

Ed utilized various species of wood with different colors to express his thoughts in this panel. None of the wood used in any panel is dyed; everything you see is the natural color of the wood. The colors Ed chose are inspired from the rainbow. At the center of the rainbow is a pastel green representing peace and it surrounds the throne of God, the Great Energy. We are part of that green quietness, the holiness around His throne. Ed says, "We are the green, unless we haven't done our homework and then we start moving towards the darkness. We don't have the wisdom and experience. We haven't joined anything together so we haven't come out of the darkness and into the light that is here." At the bottom, Adam is a darker color of red as he was made from the dust of the earth. As we go up into Eve, she is white representing the purity and whiteness of love. The female upside-down triangle is made from mahogany, a softer wood, and Eve is made of cherry, a soft, sweet wood. The pillars are made from an ornamental shrub that Ed received from a neighbor in Kalkaska, Michigan who was burning it in his wood stove

---

5 "Meaning of Numbers in the Bible: The Number 6," Bible-Study.org, , accessed December 29, 2016, http://www.bible-study.org/bibleref/meaning-of-numbers-in-bible/6.html.

6 "Meaning of Numbers in the Bible: The Number 7," Bible-Study.org, accessed December 29, 2016, http://www.bible-study.org/bibleref/meaning-of-numbers-in-bible/7.html.

to keep warm. Ed enjoyed the opportunity to represent his hometown and local environment through the wood he deliberately chose to use.

MOSES AND THE TEN COMMANDMENTS

This panel is called *Moses and the Ten Commandments* and portrays Moses after receiving the ten commandments: laws given to him by the Creator to deliver to the Israelites. *"When the LORD finished speaking with Moses on Mount Sinai, he gave him the two stone tablets inscribed with the terms of the covenant, written by the finger of God."* (Exodus 31:18)

A. This is Moses, the prophet, who led God's people out of Egypt to the Promised Land.

B. Moses is holding the Ten Commandments that were chiseled into stone by God's finger so they can never be changed. The commandments are shown here in Hebrew and are held by Moses's left and right hands. The Holy Spirit sits on the left side of God and is female. Ed explains that the Ten Commandments are God's laws for us, and laws come from the male, sitting on the right side of God. The male needs the female to help him understand the nature of the law. The female (the Holy Spirit) converts law to love for the purpose of helping us understand the law of God.

Ed created the ten commandment tablets out of thorn apple wood found throughout Michigan. He cut all of the pieces of wood he used to create the tablets out of the same board, but at different angles relative to the grain to signify that though they are much the same, they are also different, like the human male and female. The role of the male is law, wisdom, and knowledge; while the role of the female is love, hope, and faith. Through love, the female teaches the male the true value of the law.

Ed's use of thorn apple wood in this case offers us two additional symbolic references from Ed. One is that God's laws in the Ten Commandments are often considered a "thorn in our side" because they are difficult to keep. Another is that Jesus wore the crown of thorns on his head as he carried his cross to be crucified.

C. Ed uses some variation of color in Moses's gown. The whiteness in his gown symbolizes his relative closeness to God, while the darker variations symbolize that he was not a saint and that he sometimes made mistakes.

D. Moses's cape is royal and gold, signifying that he was under the direction of the true royal, which was all around him.

E. Above the head of Moses is his aura or halo with white flames coming off it representing the pureness around him.

F. Inside the aura Ed placed twelve stars joined

by ribbons that perhaps make several significant symbolic references. One is a reference to the twelve tribes of Israel that Moses represented when he went up Mount Sinai to meet with God. *"Moses then wrote down everything the LORD had said. He got up early the next morning and built an altar at the foot of the mountain and set up twelve stone pillars representing the twelve tribes of Israel."* (Exodus 24:4)

A second significant reference denotes the twelve apostles of Christ. A third references the rainbow with all the colors representing Moses's closeness to God. The colors of the rainbow never change and neither will God's laws as articulated in the Ten Commandments.

G. Next to Moses is his staff, which Ed created using Sumac, a poison-wood that grows in Michigan. He used it to signify that if you take the meaning of the law wrongly, it can poison your mind. Ed explains that God's laws are something you should actually love because He thought enough that He controls Himself, and you are supposed to get to the point where you control yourself and love yourself the same as you love God. The staff also represents the Shepherd's Crook because Moses was the shepherd that led the Israelites out of Egypt to the Promised Land. Another symbolic meaning of the staff is that it is representative of the high priest. While Moses was not a priest, his brother Aaron was, and was appointed by God to be Moses's spokesperson.

H. Moses is standing on a high cliff, or a pedestal, as the mediator appointed by God. He was not the savior, but a mediator representing the 12 tribes of Israel to negotiate a contract with God in exchange for His care, guidance, and teaching.

I. Moses is surrounded by fog high on the mountain where God called him.

J. Below the feet of Moses is the Rock of Offense—the rock that we sometimes stumble over. The Rock of Offense is mentioned in the Bible three times: *"He will be as a sanctuary,*

but a stone of stumbling and a rock of offense to both the houses of Israel, as a trap and a snare to the inhabitants of Jerusalem." (Isaiah 8:14); *"Behold, I lay in Zion a stumbling stone and rock of offense, and whoever believes on Him will not be put to shame."* (Romans 9:33); and finally, *"A stone of stumbling and a rock of offense. They stumble, being disobedient to the word, to which they also were appointed."* (1 Peter 2:8)

Ed explains that the Rock of Offense also represents Christ, the bedrock, and the one who offended man.

MY MOTHER'S LOVE

Ed named this panel series *My Mother's Love*, the series through which Ed is trying to express the love of a mother. He explains that it's not about his own mother, but about all females and his idea of what they think. Ed understood that this may be heading observers in a direction that most women may not agree with, but in his own conversations with God, God told Ed that He didn't think they would disagree. This series was created with the female in mind and what Ed perceives she was thinking at the beginning of time. This portrait represents how the female developed over the years. It is also a representation of the Holy Spirit, the spirit Ed considers to be female.

According to Ed, the main concern of the female is children—from the very beginning until now—children of various races and ages. She is concerned about the children or offspring of all animals, human or otherwise. When a female finds herself alone, she wants and needs something to love, like a cat or dog or horse. When she finds one, she runs up and kisses and hugs it and talks to it. It isn't typically in a man's nature to do so.

Ed understood the female to be more visual than the male. She loves the colors of the leaves and the colors of the rainbow. She dresses differently than the male. She may have a little flower here or a leaf there. She may wear soft pastel colors or hostile reds and blacks; color choices change with time. Ed believed that the female dresses for other females, not males. She dresses to impress her friends, not the man, because he doesn't notice anyway. He is too busy wak-

ing up, eating, grabbing his tools and heading to work, sometimes without even so much as combing his hair.

Ed explains that this particular portrait examines the various feelings of man, not from the perspective of man himself, but from the woman's perspective. The female, according to Ed, continually anticipates man's needs. She thinks that man is constantly worried that there will not be enough, so she continually wonders if everyone is okay, if there is enough food, if everyone has a place to stay and to call home, if there are enough gardens planted. While the man plows the fields, she plants the seeds, weeds the garden, and harvests the fruits and vegetables. Ed says there has always been enough. We all came from the Garden of Eden and are all related to the first Adam. God anticipated our needs and has always provided.

According to Ed, God named the female "Eve," which not only means life, but also means the "wombed" man. The female carries the promise of life, what it is, where it is, and how it moves from one generation to another. As Ed explains it, it's like when a star explodes, disintegrates, splatters, and goes out into the end of the energy and then falls back in. It is then rearranged into a new world. The same phenomenon happens at birth as what happens within our universe. Man has a difficult time grasping this abstract theory of reality. He is looking for something he knows is there but may not be clear to him. Much of reality does not make sense to man, but there is "sense" there because God created reality. He is the singular energy that needs nothing here on this earth in order to exist. Everything we see, smell, or touch was created for us, His children, to help us in our education about life and to feel at home while doing so.

When Ed pondered the story of the wise men and how they followed the star to where Christ was born, time became relevant to him. The Magi were noble, educated, and they knew how to keep time. They were aware of what was to come, so the news of Christ's birth wasn't a revelation to them; it was expected. In the Old Testament, the wise men, or Magi, appear in several different texts, including the book of Daniel. It is believed that these Magi originally came from an Eastern priestly tribe during the Medo-Persian Empire and that they were very skilled in astrology and astronomy. They were among the high-ranking advisors during the Babylonian Empire and were often sought after for their wisdom and intuition.

During this time, the Jewish people were in captivity and Daniel was elevated to prominence for his correct interpretation of the King Nebuchadnezzar's dream. The king placed Daniel in charge of the Magi, with whom he most certainly shared his understanding of the scriptures and the promise of the Messiah to come. Thousands of years later, it is believed, the Magi that followed the star and brought their entourage with them on their journey to find the new Messiah and to worship him. Ed explains that understanding the rhythm in space and the fact that all things work together, allows one to actually chart time and space, which is what the wise men did to find Jesus.[7]

This panel series is divided into sections: above and below the line, and left and right of center.

Above the line, and in each panel except the first, Ed placed a type of star symbol, each with special meaning. Ed utilized numerology and sacred geometry to express his thought pattern for each of the stars.

7 John MacArthur, "Who Were the Wise Men?" Grace to You, February 05, 1978, accessed February 8, 2017, https://www.gty.org/library/sermons-library/2182/who-were-the-wise-men.

Below and to the left of Jesus are the kings, wise men, and shepherds who were called and knew what they were looking for. To the right of Jesus are villagers and families learning and teaching their children what has happened, how to make sense of it, and what to do.

Ed depicted the people in this series with different skin tones and colors to represent the numerous races of people from all over the world who came to see the newborn king.

PANEL ONE

A. At the top of the first panel, there is no star, which Ed designed purposefully to symbolize God. The number one is singular and sepa-

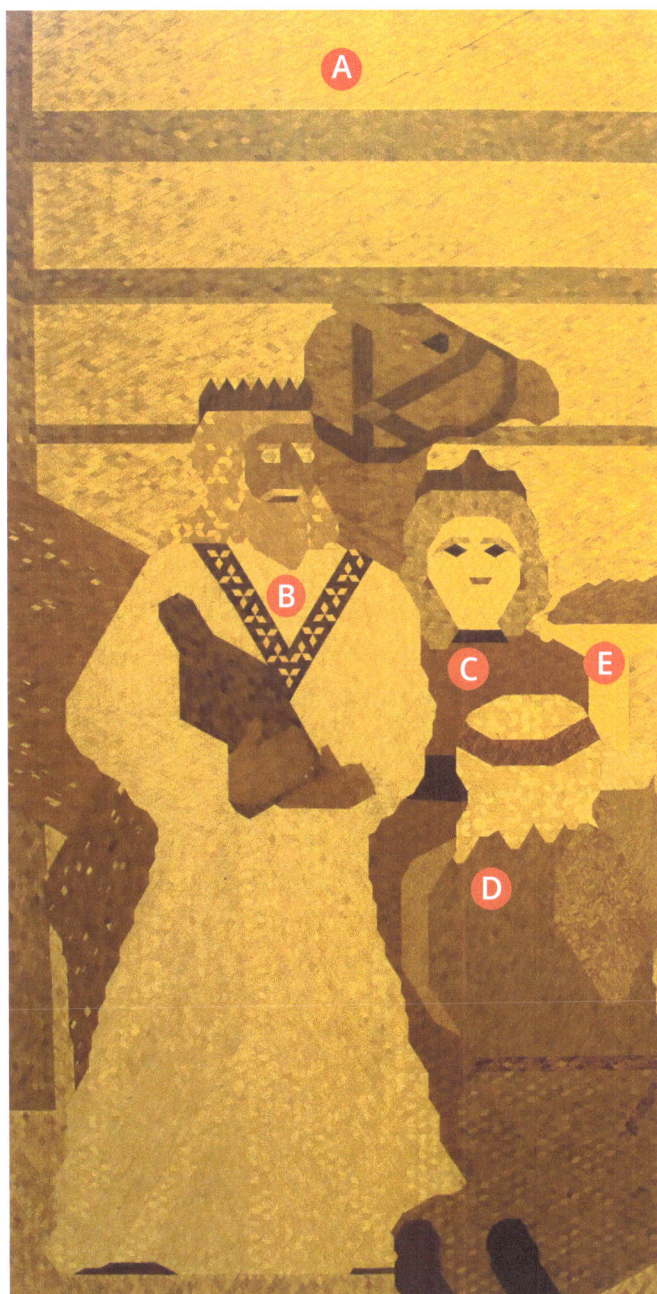

rate from the multitudes. It is both male and female, odd and even, the beginning and the end.

Ed also says that the number one is a "useless" number. Exploring this concept further, it is possible Ed says this because the number one is not a prime number. From the Prime FAQ page of the website *www.primes.utm.edu*, Chris K. Caldwell answers the question, "Why is the number one not prime?", by saying that, by definition: "An integer greater than one is called a prime number if its only positive divisors (factors) are one and itself." [8] Caldwell goes on to explain the following:

> In discussion of warfare you often hear the phrase "divide and conquer." The same principle holds in mathematics. Many of the properties of an integer can be traced back to the properties of its prime divisors, allowing us to divide the problem (literally) into smaller problems. **The number one is useless** in this regard because $a = 1 \cdot a = 1 \cdot 1 \cdot a = ...$ That is, divisibility by one fails to provide us any information about a. [9]

B. Pictured in this panel is one of the Magi, or a king, coming to verify the Messiah is born and bringing a gift he carries in front of his heart.

C. With the king is his wife, who is always with him. According to Ed's research, the king is chosen by his own people to be their ruler. He is allowed one year to find a bride and she remains with him all the time. If she cannot have an offspring within that one year, she loses her position and the king then finds another woman. If the king and his wife do conceive an offspring within the year, they never separate from then on.

D. Below the king's wife is the torch bearer who advises him on how he should rule his country.

E. The flame of his torch represents the Holy Spirit, who advises us all on how to rule our lives. The flame is pointing toward the newborn King, baby Jesus.

PANEL TWO

The next panel should be a representation of the number two, but Ed purposely left out the number two because he says it has no value and does not multiply properly. Exploring the history of numbers further, it is from the Greek philosopher and mathematician Pythagoras that much of number symbolism was generated. According to Pythagoras, numbers had masculine and feminine meanings. "Odd numbers were considered masculine; even numbers feminine because they are weaker than the odd. Unlike the odd, even numbers when divided have nothing in the center. Further, the odd numbers are the master, because an odd number + an even number always results in an odd number. And two evens can never produce an odd, while two odds produce an even. Since the birth of a son was considered more fortunate than the birth of a daughter, odd numbers became associated with good luck." [10]

Further explanation relative to Pythagoras and the number two comes from the text, "The Secret Teachings Of All Ages":

> The following symbolic names were given to the duad--2--because it has been divided, and is two rather than one; and when there are two, each is opposed to the other: genius, evil, darkness, inequality, instability, movability, boldness, fortitude, contention, matter, dissimilarity, partition between multitude and monad, defect, shapelessness, indefiniteness, indeterminateness, harmony, tolerance, root, feet of fountain-abounding idea, top, Phanes, opinion, fallacy, alterity, diffidence, impulse, death, motion, generation, mutation, division, longitude, augmentation, composition, communion, misfortune, sustentation, imposition, marriage, soul,

8 Chris K. Caldwell, "Why is the number one not prime?" The Prime Pages, accessed February 8, 2017, https://primes.utm.edu/notes/faq/one.html.

9 Chris K. Caldwell, "Why is the number one not prime?" The Prime Pages, accessed February 8, 2017, https://primes.utm.edu/notes/faq/one.html.

10 Paul A. Calter, Squaring the Circle: Geometry in Art and Architecture (John Wiley, 2008).

and science.[11]

A. On top of the second panel is a three-pointed star representing the Trinity—Father, Son, and Holy Spirit.

B. Below the star are the three kings that traveled from afar to verify the birth of the Messiah.

C. The three kings came bearing gifts. According to the article, "Why Did the Magi Bring Gold,

11 Manly P. Hall, "Pythagorean Mathematics," Secret Teachings of All Ages: Pythagorean Mathematics, accessed February 8, 2017, http://www.sacred-texts.com/eso/sta/sta16.htm.

Frankincense and Myrrh?," the author explains, "These valuable items were standard gifts to honor a king or deity in the ancient world: gold as a precious metal, frankincense as perfume or incense, and myrrh as anointing oil."[12]

The names of the three kings are not known. In fact, there may have been more than three men, who were perhaps also kings, in the entourage traveling with them. It is believed that there were three wise men, kings, Magi, because that is the number of gifts bestowed on the new King. They learned about the coming of the Messiah back in the days of the Old Testament and knew that he was on his way when God led them with a bright light to where he was in the manger.

D. Like in the first panel, the flame of the torch is leaning toward the newborn king, Jesus.

PANEL THREE

A At the top of the third panel is a square with four corners that Ed designed to represent Solomon's second temple, otherwise known as Herod's Temple. It is the temple where Jesus worshiped and also the temple where He drove out the moneychangers and traders selling sacrificial animals.

Solomon's Temple had several sections, or chambers within it.

B. The outer courtyard was the Court of the Gentiles, where trading and money changing took place. To go beyond this point inside the temple you had to be a purified Jew. No gentiles were allowed in.

C. The second chamber was known as the Court of Women.

D. The third chamber was the Court of Men or the Court of Israel.

E. The fourth area, known as the Court of Priests, was a sacred area where the altar

12 "Why Did the Magi Bring Gold, Frankincense and Myrrh?" Biblical Archaeology Society, accessed March 05, 2017, https://www.biblicalarchaeology.org/daily/people-cultures-in-the-bible/jesus-historical-jesus/why-did-the-magi-bring-gold-frankincense-and-myrrh/.

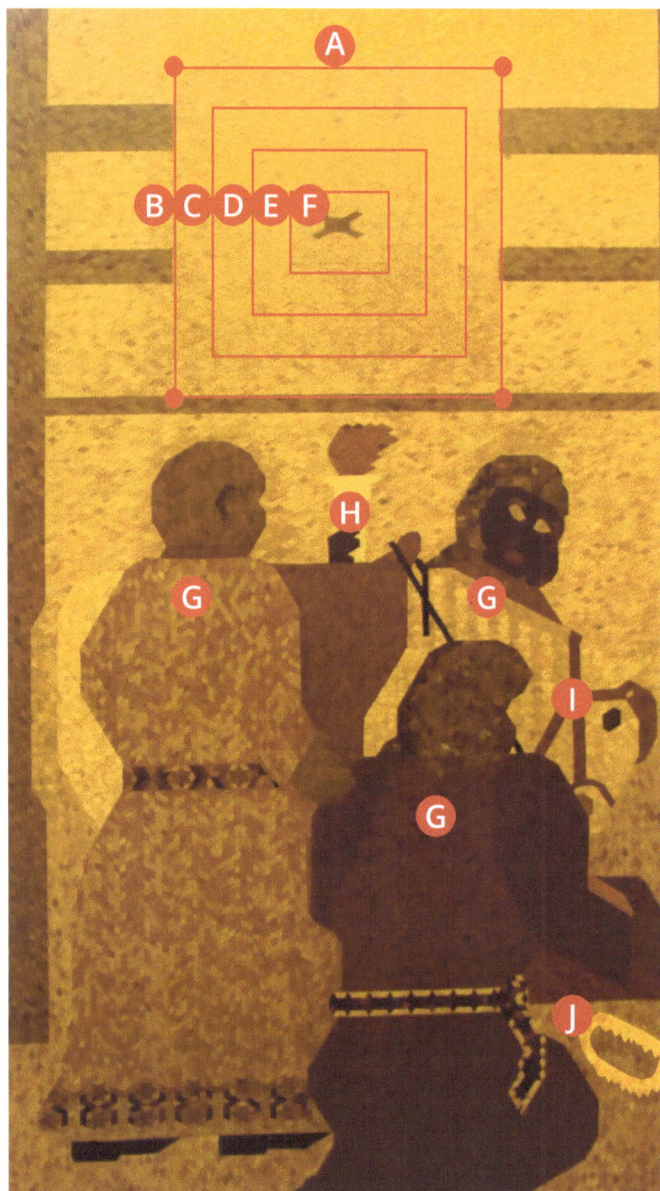

I. The horse is also bowing in reverence for the newborn king.

J. The king on his knees has placed his crown on the ground, laying it down before the throne of the Lord.

PANEL FOUR

A. At the top of the center panel is a five-pointed star, representing the Star of Bethlehem. Ed explains it was not a common star, but a kind of torch in the sky leading the Magi to Bethlehem to witness the birth of the Messiah. Once they worshiped the newborn king and gave their gifts, the star led them out of Bethlehem a different way from which they came so Herod could not find them.

B. Below the star is Joseph and the virgin Mary looking down at the newborn son she bore.

C. In the cradle is baby Jesus, the fulfillment of numerous Old Testament prophecies, including Isaiah 7:14 which states, *"Therefore the Lord himself will give you a sign: Behold, the virgin shall conceive and bear a son, and shall call his name Immanuel."*

D. Surrounding baby Jesus are three shepherds who were told by an angel of the Lord that a Savior, the Messiah, was born and is wrapped in clothes, lying in a manger. *"So they hurried off and found Mary and Joseph, and the baby, who was lying in the manger. When they had seen him, they spread the word concerning what had been told them about this child, and all who heard it were amazed at what the shepherds said to them. But Mary treasured up all these things and pondered them in her heart. The shepherds returned, glorifying and praising God for all the things they had heard and seen, which were just as they had been told."* (Luke 2:16-20)[13]

E. The staffs on the ground are what the shepherds walked with to help them navigate the stony ground. They also used

stood and animals were sacrificed.

F. In the center was the Holy of Holies, a place where only the High Priests were allowed and only on the day of atonement to offer sacrifice for the entire nation. This is where God dwelled and it was separated from the Court of the Priests by a thick veil, shielding God from the sins of man.

G. Below the square are more kings who came to witness the birth of Jesus. Again, their various skin tones represent the numerous races and nationalities present from across the world.

H. The torch bearer's flame is leaning toward the newborn king.

13 "The Birth of Jesus," Luke 2 - Bible Gateway, accessed March 5, 2017, https://www.biblegateway.com/passage/?search=Luke%2B2.

them to defend themselves while shepherding their sheep.

PANEL FIVE

A. At the top of the fifth panel is a six-pointed star. Ed explains that the number six represents perfection, and he placed it here because the law has now changed with the birth of Jesus. Before him, the law was imperfect, and now the law has changed to include the new king that we are to worship and he is perfect.

The following excerpt is taken from the book,

The Theology of Arithmetic; Number Symbolism in Platonism and Early Christianity, that explains more on the number six:

A good example is found in one of Philo's best-known texts, "On the Creation", in which he argues for the intellectual coherence, even superiority, of Moses's account of the creation. Near the beginning of the treatise Philo explains why God is said to have created the world in six days. It is not as if God, who conceived and executed everything all at once, needed the extra time. Rather, in those six days God supplied order and rank to created beings. According to the laws of the nature of numbers, six is the number most conducive to begetting. Philo explains:

'For it is the first perfect number after the monad, equal to its parts and composed by them (half is a triad, a third is a dyad, a sixth is a monad). And it is, so to speak, male and female, fitted together by the power of each. For in things that exist odd is male and even is female. So the beginning of odd numbers is the triad, and of even numbers the dyad, but the power of both is the hexad. For the world, being the most perfect of created things, was put together in accordance with the perfect number, the hexad. And since it was about to have in itself things created from copulation, it had to be fashioned in accordance with a mixed number, the first even-odd. It was to encompass the form of the male, who sows the seed, and that of the female, who receives offspring.'

In this excerpt from *"On the Creation,"* Philo presents several number symbols, some of which he assumes his readers know and accept. The first pertains to six. In antiquity, perfect numbers were those equal to the sum of their factors (including the number one). Hence six, whose factors are one, two, and three, is a perfect number. The second symbol pertains to the numbers two and three. All numbers were considered to have gender: even numbers were female, and odd numbers, starting with three, were male. (The number one was frequently considered

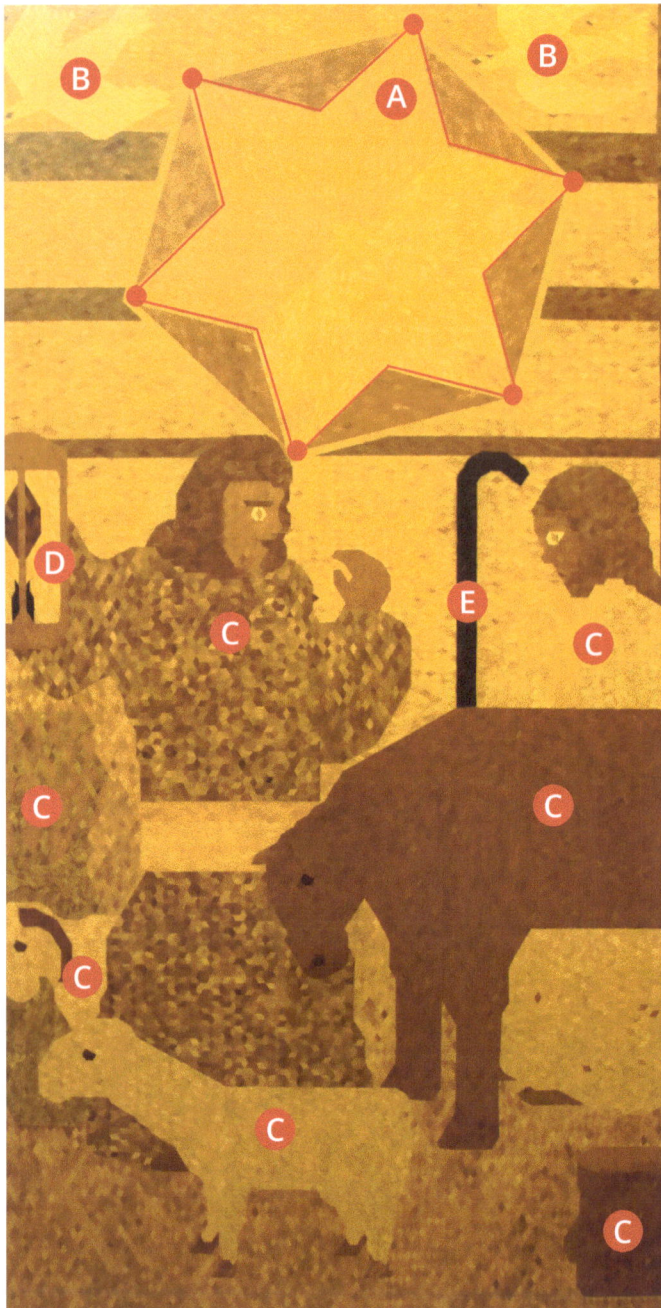

numbers, both here and throughout his writings, to unite seemingly disparate worlds."[14]

Another explanation Ed gives for using this particular six-pointed star is that it represents family. He designed this star with a 7-degree tilt to signify that some families do not always get along, and are not perfect.

B. On each side of the six-pointed star are doves, a symbol of the Holy Spirit, plus peace and love.

C Below the star is the torchbearer and his son, along with several animals. Ed explains that this panel represents the sacrifices that each family had to make each year to follow God's laws every day in order to be forgiven and to communicate with him. The sacrificial lamb, the goat, the bag of barley for flour, the cow and the pail of milk are all there. It was a hardship on each family to keep these laws, but since the crucifixion of Christ, families no longer are required to follow these particular laws to communicate with God.

D. The torchbearer is carrying a lantern that is closed with a very dim light, which Ed designed to signify that this form of sacrifice is now ceasing.

E. The torchbearer's son is holding his staff while learning the job of caring for their flock.

PANEL SIX

A. On the sixth panel, Ed designed a seven-pointed star to symbolize that the number seven represents spiritual perfection, and is said to be inspired by the Holy Spirit.

According to *The Companion Bible*, "SEVEN Denotes spiritual perfection. It is the number or hallmark of the Holy Spirit's work. He is the Author of God's Word, and seven is stamped on it as the watermark is seen in the manufacture of paper. He is the Author and Giver

androgynous.) The gendering of number was both extensive and old, going back to Aristotle and the Pythagoreans. These assumptions explain Philo's observation that six is the first number born from the multiplicative union of male and female numbers. So it makes sense that the creation happened in six days: no other number better typifies the fertility God implemented in the natural order. Philo builds upon both of these number symbols, one illustrating perfection and the other sexual generation, to argue that to be perfect and productive, creation had to have occurred in six days. Philo uses

14 Joel Kalvesmaki, "Generating the World of Numbers: Pythagorean and Platonist Number Symbolism in the First Century," Generating the World of Numbers: Pythagorean and Platonist Number Symbolism in the First Century, accessed February 07, 2017, https://chs.harvard.edu/CHS/article/display/6304.

of life; and seven is the number which regulates every period of incubation and gestation, in insects, birds, animals, and man."[15]

B. Ed believed that the Holy Spirit is female, and this panel, with the name *My Mother's Love* on it, represents the female thought pattern and the way the female feels and relates to life.

C. Below the star is a family, including a father, mother, son, and grandmother. The son hangs his head because he brought a black sheep as a sacrifice, which is not proper. But

15 E. W. Bullinger, "The Spiritual Significance of Numbers," The Rain.org, accessed October 7, 2017, http://www.therain. org/appendixes/app10.html.

instead of the father and mother correcting the son, it is the mother and grandmother correcting and teaching him, which Ed explains is not the way a family should function. Proper instruction should come from the mother and father. Ed also says he was considered to be the black sheep in his own family.

D. The torch held by the father is pointing toward the newborn king.

PANEL SEVEN

A. On the last panel, there is no number present. Ed chose not to use the number eight because as he said, "It is always an even number." Ed also left off the number nine because it symbolizes divine completeness. Ed explains that he still has work to do, so he left it off.

B. At the top of this panel are two angels blowing their trumpets to announce to the shepherds that the Messiah is born. *"And there were shepherds living out in the fields nearby, keeping watch over their flocks at night. An angel of the Lord appeared to them, and the glory of the Lord shone around them, and they were terrified. But the angel said to them, 'Do not be afraid. I bring you good news that will cause great joy for all the people. Today in the town of David a Savior has been born to you; he is the Messiah, the Lord. This will be a sign to you: You will find a baby wrapped in cloths and lying in a manger.' Suddenly a great company of the heavenly host appeared with the angel, praising God and saying, 'Glory to God in the highest heaven, and on earth peace to those on whom his favor rests.' When the angels had left them and gone into heaven, the shepherds said to one another, 'Let's go to Bethlehem and see this thing that has happened, which the Lord has told us about.'"* (Luke 2:8-20)

C. Below the angels is a torchbearer whose flame is leaning toward the new born king.

D. A proper mold of a family is present, with mother, father, son, and daughter. The mother and father are both instructing their children because they have equal responsibility to them, and the children have equal responsibility to their parents.

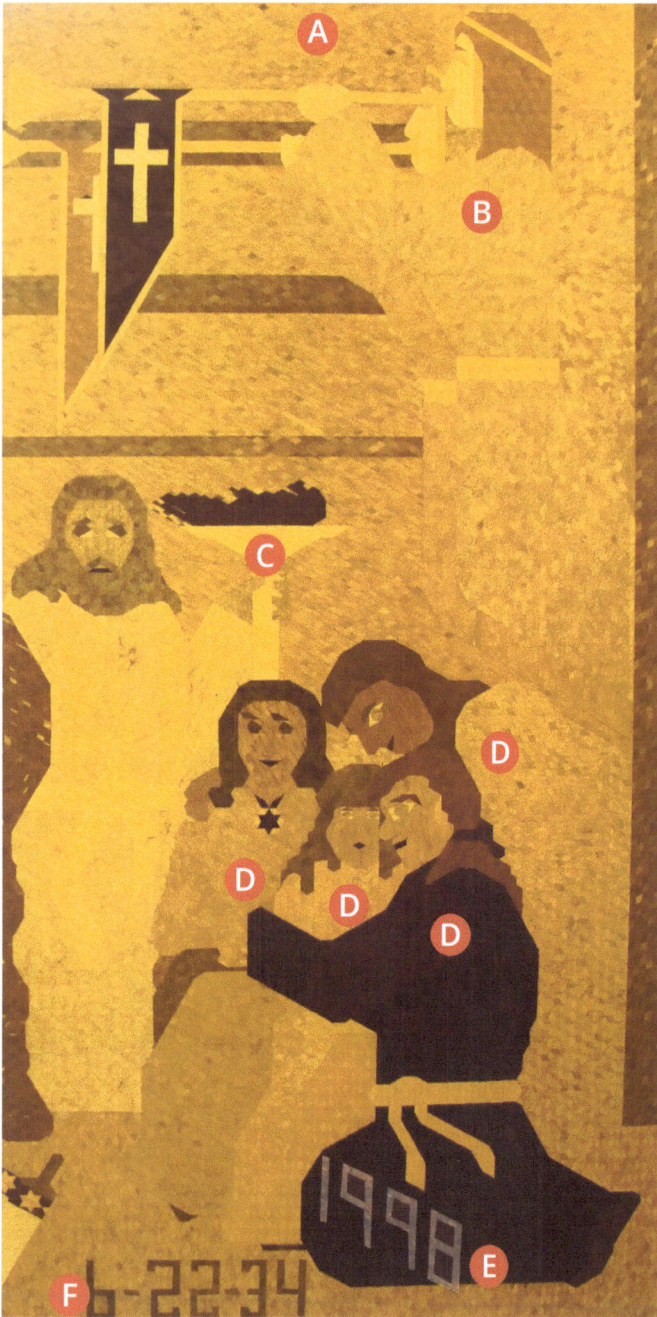

E. At the bottom of the robe of the son, the number 1998 is present to represent the year this panel series was made.

F. Ed's artistic signature is at the bottom of the panel: 6-22-34.

MY FATHER'S LOVE

Ed's amazing journey began with this seven-panel series he named *My Father's Love*. He created this series in a very small workshop while living in Orlando, Florida. Each panel is 4-feet by 8-feet, so he could create only one panel at a time in the limited space. Ed started with the center panel of Jesus, with the first piece placed in the throat (or voice box) of Jesus. Once completed, he moved this panel out of the shop and began work on the next panel. He did not create them in sequence, and he never saw them put together until they were assembled and displayed for the first time. Ed couldn't believe they actually fit together perfectly and said, "Wow! I think I did exactly what I was supposed to do."

Where *My Mother's Love* series represents the female perspective, this series represents the male perspective—the male way of thinking or thought pattern, which Ed suggests he was much more comfortable with.

Ed explains that this series has a lot of love in it. He says, "Love is what is going to cause the earth to change, people on earth to change, when they realize what love does for them."

Ed dedicated this series to his fathers, both his heavenly father and his human father. He says there are many people who don't know their fathers at all and he hopes this series helps them become grounded in thought that they do have a father that loves them.

This series depicts a supper, but not a copy of the one Leonardo da Vinci created in his famous painting of *The Last Supper*. This is Ed's version of

what he perceived happened that night. It includes the same cast of characters as the Leonardo painting, but placed in a different order. Ed claimed that he did not have a copy of any picture to go by, so he simply relied on his own thought pattern to develop the story told herein.

Ed referred to the event in this image as a Seder, a Jewish ritual feast that marks the beginning of the Jewish holiday of Passover. To Ed, this is Jesus's Seder where Jesus told his disciples to remember him and what he did because he was going away. Jesus told his disciples, *"Do this in remembrance of me."* He wanted them to remember what his life was like; remember that he lived as they did, ate as they did.

Ed believed that women and children were actually present at the last supper because it was a tradition that they be present at a Seder.

This is a portrait, not only of Christ, but also of the apostles and how they lived and died. We all know how Christ died but most of us know very little about the apostles and how they were martyred for preaching Christ's message. Ed says, "They could have escaped, they could have run away, but they didn't. They did their jobs in various parts of the world. Some stayed in Jerusalem, but most of them went out as missionaries, picking their respective countries and traveling there to preach and telling about the fact that the Messiah has come."

According to Ed, it was very difficult to discover the history behind each of the apostles because so little was written about them, but he proved that it is there if you search hard enough.

Ed determined the order of the apostles from left to right as pictured in the series in a manner designed to help tell the story from his perspective. He claimed there is rhythm to every story and he was deliberately trying to keep up this rhythm through the order he chose. This is not a historical representation of the last supper, but Ed's own thought pattern of how he saw the story unfold. According to Ed, "Before you start a portrait, you have to really sit down and think about what you are trying to say through the way you put everything together. And with the color harmonics and symbols and the individuals' personalities as tools to make the truth a little clearer, you must make choices. I chose this particular meal to tell the story from my perspective."

A great deal of thinking and planning went into each panel to capture the essence of the story. The colors and types of wood used in the arrangements and the garments of the apostles all have meaning. As Ed reminds us, simply consider the order in the very simple rainbow of seven colors —they are pastels and they are set at certain distances from one another. Ed chose the colors and designs for each garment based on how the apostles perceived themselves and how Ed understood their history. It was important to Ed that he capture their individual demeanors, what they actually did, and how they thought. In this depiction of the Seder, the apostles are all dressed in their traveling clothes.

Ed was also aware that there were multiple languages represented so he included them in this series, including Greek, Hebrew, and Anglo-Saxon. Various words in these languages carry the same meaning, and symbols help to tell the story.

According to Ed, 300 to 400 years after the ascension of Christ—and because of the confusion surrounding the apostles—the earliest artists began using symbols to represent each of the apostles, focusing in particular on how they died. Each one of them was killed uniquely, and the way each apostle died told much about what they each taught their listeners about the Messiah.

Upon looking at the panels straight on, one will notice the series is divided into three sections: top, middle, and bottom.

TOP: There are words and symbols above the apostles that have multiple meanings. Ed placed the words to the left of Jesus to represent what the apostles needed at that time. To the right of Jesus are words written in Greek and Anglo-Saxon, and they have special meaning to Ed.

MIDDLE: Across the middle of the panel series, on the front of the table cover on which they dined, is a musical scale that Ed called the sound of the universe, the song without words. Ed understood that scriptures were put into musical song and sung by little children long before they were placed in book form.

BOTTOM: Along the bottom of the series of panels are symbols representing how each apostle was martyred or particular actions for which they were especially revered. There are words and symbols that represent some of the traditions and rituals that took place at that particular Seder. There are also some that simply have very personal meaning to Ed.

PANEL ONE

A. THOMAS DIDYMUS: The first apostle in the series is Thomas Didymus, better known as Doubting Thomas. He stands at the end of the table talking about his doubts. John 20:24-25 says, *"Now Thomas (also known as Didymus), one of the Twelve, was not with the disciples when Jesus came. So the other disciples told him, 'We have seen the Lord!' But he said to them, 'Unless I see the nail marks in his hands and put my finger where the nails were, and put my hand into his side, I will not believe.'"* (NIV)

B. Above the head of Thomas is the word FAITH, which Ed placed there to signify that he needed more faith to remove his doubt. Once Jesus let Thomas put his finger into the wound on His hand, Thomas declared, *"My Lord and my God,"* and his doubt became great faith.

C. On Thomas's garment are designs of bees. According to *symbols.ehibou.com*, "In Christian symbolism it {a bee} represents the immor-

E. ANDREW: The second apostle shown is Andrew. He was the brother of Simon Peter and they were fishermen. *"As Jesus was walking beside the Sea of Galilee, he saw two brothers, Simon called Peter and his brother Andrew. They were casting a net into the lake, for they were fishermen. 'Come, follow me,' Jesus said, 'and I will send you out to fish for people.'"* (Matthew 4:18-19)

F. Above Andrew's head is the word HOPE. According to Ed, Andrew needed more hope.

G. Under Andrew is an X, symbolizing how he was crucified. While preaching in Patra, Greece, Andrew was arrested and condemned to die on the cross. He begged to be crucified on a different type of cross than was Jesus because he didn't feel worthy to die the same way, so they hung him on an X-shaped cross, now known as Saint Andrew's Cross. People jeered at him and spit on him while he hung there for three days and nights, preaching the gospel, until he finally died of starvation, lack of water, and heat exhaustion. Before he expired, he asked God to forgive the individuals who crucified him, just as Jesus did.

H. Above the X, you can see Andrew's robe, but not his feet. Ed explains that Andrew's feet do not touch the ground because of his spiritual teachings. Ed explains, "He is not connected to the dirt that Adam was, he is not dust of the Earth, he is special in my perception."

I. Under Andrew's chin is a beautiful geometric scarf or portion of his garment. If one looks closely, Andrew's scarf also looks like a crown sitting on top of the head of someone sitting in a chair facing Andrew. Ed suggests that this might be an image of the Old Testament prophet Elijah sitting in what is known as Elijah's Chair.

A significant Jewish traditional symbol is to provide an empty chair for the prophet Elijah in case he comes to be a witness at circumcisions when the sign of the covenant is placed upon the body of the child.[17]

Another Jewish tradition associated with

tality of soul and signifies the resurrection. During three months of winter it seems to disappear as Christ was dead for three days before his resurrection. The bee's sting was associated with the Judgment Day. It is also a sign of wisdom."[16]

D. Under Thomas's arm are two arrows and below his feet is a spear, symbols of how he most likely died. According to Ed's research, he was run through with a spear, hit by arrows, and then stoned to death.

16 "Bee", Symbols, October 14, 2015, accessed January 5, 2017, http://symbols.ehibou.com/bee/.

17 "Elijah, Chair of," Jewish Virtual Library, accessed January 7, 2017, http://www.jewishvirtuallibrary.org/elijah-chair-of.

the Seder meal during Passover is to leave an empty place setting and cup on the table, and leave the door open to invite in the prophet Elijah. "No one really knows exactly when or where the expectation that Elijah would return on Passover began, but it has nonetheless been a long-standing tradition to set an extra place at the table in anticipation of his return. Even the wine is poured for him as the celebrants fill their own cups for the third cup of wine. Jews the world over believe that Elijah will come on the eve of Passover as a forerunner to the Messiah, and that he will answer all questions and resolve all debates over the Torah."[18]

J. On the back of the chair is a symbolic X combined with a cross that forms a head at the top. "The Chi-Rho (pronounced "KEE-roe") is a Christian symbol consisting of the intersection of the capital Greek letters Chi (X) and Rho (P), which are the first two letters of the word "Christ" in Greek (ΧΡΙΣΤΟΣ, Christos). The Chi-Rho can represent either Christ or Christianity and is also known as a Christogram, a monogram for the name of Christ in Greek."[19]

PANEL TWO

A. BARTHOLOMEW: The third apostle from left to right is Bartholomew, also known as Nathanael. You can barely see his face except for one eye. Ed displayed him this way to represent how he was made a martyr.

B. Bartholomew refused to recant his proclamation that Christ was the risen Son of God, so he was flayed, or skinned alive. The three knives beneath him on the table symbolize the means of death.

C. Above Bartholomew's head reads, "GOD IS LOVE." Ed says this statement is tied to FAITH and HOPE from the first panel. Ed is suggesting here that we can only have faith in what we believe. He explains that we are too far away from when the resurrection oc-

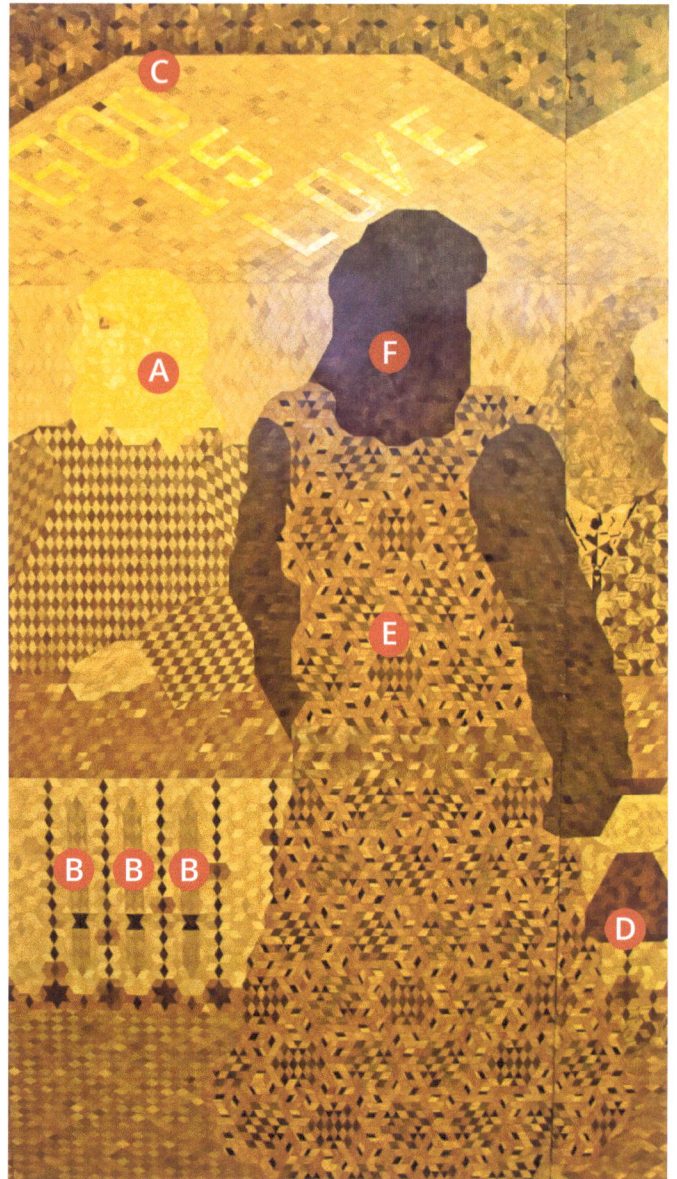

curred to have any actual evidence; we have only a personal feeling; but Ed believed we have that challenge to face in all aspects of life.

D. JUDAS: The fourth apostle has his back to us; and he is hiding his bag of money under the table and away from Jesus. This is Judas, the traitor who betrayed Jesus for 30 silver coins. His symbol is the money bag, which Ed made royal in color to signify that it was the King's money.

E. Ed calls the pattern he created on Judas's garment "confusion" because that was his thought pattern at the time: no logic, reason, or rationale. Judas was thought to be crazy, but Ed believed that Judas was merely misled. In fact, Ed claimed that he is Judas in this

18 "Elijah," A Virtual Passover - Elijah, accessed January 5, 2017, http://avirtualpassover.com/elijah.htm.

19 "Chi Rho," ReligionFacts, October 29, 2016, accessed October 14, 2017, http://www.religionfacts.com/chi-rho.

panel. "Judas did not accept the fact, and I did not accept the fact either, that some of the things we did or that we became, we were forced to do or become simply to stay alive; so, in that way I was Judas too."

Judas hung himself after he betrayed Jesus, but Ed says he died twice. After he kissed Jesus, he left and headed home. He suddenly realized that what he did was wrong and was a terrible sin, so he went back to the temple to give the money back. The priest would not accept the money back, so Judas felt so remorseful that he went out on the hill and hung himself.

Ed explains that the rope broke after breaking Judas's neck but Judas wasn't dead yet, and he fell down the cliff into the garbage pit that was always burning. Everyone that lived in Jerusalem took their garbage there and threw it over the cliff where fire continually burned the trash. This is where Judas finally died.

According to Ed, when the priest would not accept the money back, Judas threw it on the floor and left. Considered blood money, the priest refused to put it back into the treasury. Instead, it went into a general fund which was used to purchase the field where Judas was thought to have committed suicide. This field became the burial place for individuals with no one to bury them, and it was called Potter's Field. Ed talks about how his own father wanted to make sure that none of his children ended up buried in a Potter's Field. He explains when he was around four years old, his parents took him to the cemetery in Kalkaska and showed him his future burial spot for when he himself should die. This is where Ed's oldest daughter is now buried. Ed knew that upon his own death, he had a burial place next to his daughter, his dad, and his little brother; not in a Potter's Field.

PANEL THREE

A. PETER: Next is the apostle Simon Peter, brother of Andrew and the leader of the twelve Apostles. He was the first to declare that Jesus was the Son of God, and he was the one who denied knowing Jesus three times when pressed by the authorities.

B. Peter was crucified upside down on an inverted cross, just the way he requested, because, like Thomas, Peter felt unworthy to be crucified as Christ was. Ed notes that Peter was also tied to the cross, not nailed The symbol of an inverted cross is below Peter to represent how he died.

C. Above Peter's head is a faint image of a cherub, one of two that appear on either side of Jesus, the covenant. As described in Exodus 25, there were two cherubs on the Ark of

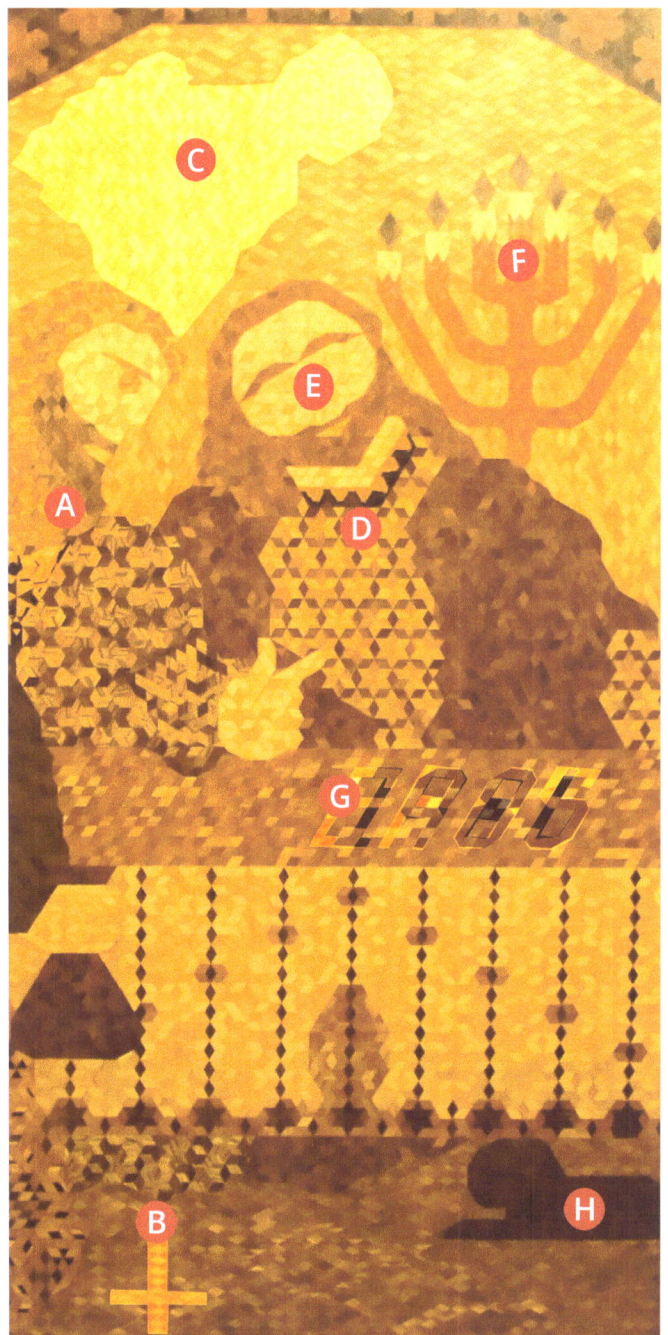

the Covenant, one on each end, facing each other, their wings spread to shield the cover placed atop the Ark with God's pact placed inside. Only the High Priests knew what the cherubs looked like, which is why Ed made them from wood the same color as the background, so they could not be easily seen.

Ed explains that the cherubs also represent the women who served at the table on the night of the last supper and who needed to be recognized. If one studies the reverse image of each cherub, Ed suggests a female head in profile or an older woman who served at the last Seder of Jesus may be visable.

D. JOHN: Next to Peter is John, known as the disciple whom Jesus loved. John is the only apostle that lived a long life and died of natural causes. He was persecuted throughout his life for proclaiming that Jesus was the Messiah, and was exiled on the Island of Patmos. John authored the Gospel of John, I John, II John, III John, and Revelations, the last book of the Bible. Ed says he was known as the apostle of love and he loved Christ. During the last supper, John leaned on Christ's bosom while being fed by him.

E. John the Apostle in the panel has no pupils in his eyes. The same is true of Jesus depicted in the next panel. Ed explains that the eyes are the windows of the soul, and the absence of colors in the eyes of both John and Christ offer the closest one can get to "knowing" the pure souls of Christ and John as living human beings. As Ed perceived it, Jesus was without sin and there was no darkness in him at all. John was closest to Jesus, which is why their eyes are so similar.

F. Over John's right shoulder is the seven-branch menorah. According to the commandment in Exodus 25:31-40, the seven-branch menorah symbolizes the seven days of creation, with the center light representing the Sabbath. It is also said to symbolize the burning bush as seen by Moses on Mount Horeb (Exodus 3).

G. On the table in front of John, an observer will find the year 1986, the year Ed completed *My Father's Love*. If one looks at the year at a

severe angle, one may recognize the word "EROS" which is the Hebrew word for love. Ed claims that Eros denotes the highest form of human love.

H. Below John is a small black lamb. Ed offers up several reasons for its symbolic significance. First, a small black lamb represents the sinless Lamb of God. In the Old Testament, lambs were animals often sacrificed to atone for sins. When Jesus died on the cross to atone for all our sins, he became the sacrificial Lamb of God. Second, the lamb in the color black symbolizes rejection. The term "black sheep" is often used to describe someone who is odd and doesn't fit in with a group or family and is often rejected. Jesus, who was rejected and crucified, was considered a black sheep. Ed also considered himself a black sheep and claims this lamb also represents him. Third, the black sheep symbolizes the Paschal Lamb. In the Book of Exodus, God told Moses to instruct the Israelites to take an unblemished lamb into their homes, and on the fourth day, sacrifice it and eat it, then sprinkle the blood of the lamb on the door posts to protect them from the last plague, the death of every firstborn son. Fourth, Ed claims that the lamb is the female lion, the Aslan of the Tribe of Judah. The name "Aslan" is Turkish for "lion" and is the name of the lion that represent Jesus, in C.S. Lewis's *The Lion the Witch and the Wardrobe*. The symbol for the Tribe of Judah is a lion, referenced in the Book of Genesis 49:9. The Lion of Judah is also referenced in the Book of Revelation 5:5 where it says, "*And one of the elders saith unto me, Weep not: behold, the Lion of the tribe of Judah, the Root of David, hath prevailed to open the book, and to loose the seven seals thereof.*"

PANEL FOUR

A. JESUS: The central panel in the series is depicting Jesus, the very first panel Ed created. The first diamond he placed is beneath Jesus's beard. Ed believed Jesus was also an apostle at the Seder meal that night. He was declared an apostle in the Book of Psalms, and he was the apostle of the Great Energy, a priest of the most high. Jesus is in the center of the portrait because that is where he belongs, in the center of all time and all eternity. Ed embraced Jesus as his own apostle and viewed Jesus as an apostle to the entire world, according to the foretelling in the Old Testament.

B. At the top center of the panel, beneath the border, is one dark-colored diamond that may seem out of place. Ed placed it there to signify that we are human and we all make mistakes.

C. Above Jesus's head on each side of his halo are two doves. Ed explains they are angels that are always with Jesus and they are shadowing him, protecting him as he was set apart. Like the cherubim that shadowed the Ark of the Covenant, in Hebrew 9:5: *"And over it the cherubims of glory shadowing the mercyseat; of which we cannot now speak particularly,"* doves are symbols of the Holy Spirit sent to protect Mary so that she would conceive and give birth to the son of God—*"The angel answered, "The Holy Spirit will come on you, and the power of the Most High will overshadow you. So the holy one to be born will be called the Son of God."* (Luke 1:35)

D. The halo around Jesus's head is what Ed calls his aura. Ed explains that you get your aura from your own personal thought pattern escaping the brain; it is an electrical aura around you. According to Ed, if you pay attention, you can tell a person's thoughts and motivations by watching his aura. A golden aura is said to mean, "You are connected to higher power or God, and that you are inspired, devoted, and are coming to a time of revitalization. It is a color of higher mind, understanding of the patterns of the Universe and of the laws of the Universe."[20] While Christians do not practice this anymore, Ed thinks it was relevant in Christianity at the time.

The debate about auras and halos described in the Bible, and found in images associated with Christianity, is ongoing. Many believe the word "halo" is not mentioned in the Bible, and as such is a pagan symbol. Halos appeared abundantly in paintings of Jesus around the 4th century, and on images of the saints, including the Virgin Mary, throughout the Middle Ages. There is, however, only one mention in scripture that includes the word "halo" in its translation: *"From what appeared to be his waist up, he looked like gleaming amber, flickering like a fire. And from his waist down, he looked like a burning flame, shining with splendor. All around him was a glowing halo, like a rainbow*

20 "The Meaning of Aura Colors," Chakra Anatomy, , accessed January 9, 2017, http://www.chakra-anatomy.com/aura-colors.html.

shining in the clouds on a rainy day. This is what the glory of the LORD looked like to me. When I saw it, I fell face down on the ground, and I heard someone's voice speaking to me." (Ezekiel 1:27-28)

E. Jesus has no eyes, signifying that he is without sin. As Ed mentioned before with the Apostle John, the eyes are the window to the soul, and the darker they are, the farther away they are from Christ. Jesus had no "darkness" in him, which is why Ed created him with no eyes.

F. The robe Jesus is wearing is purple, indicating he is the king. Only royalty were allowed to wear the color purple.

G. Jesus's hands are open and welcoming. On his right hand, he is wearing a ring represented by a square piece of wood. This is one of three squares Ed placed within the panels to pay tribute to his father who taught him the art of marquetry.

H. Between Jesus's hands is a loaf of bread and a chalice, representing his body and his blood. *"While they were eating, Jesus took bread, and when he had given thanks, he broke it and gave it to his disciples, saying, 'Take and eat; this is my body.' Then he took a cup, and when he had given thanks, he gave it to them, saying, 'Drink from it, all of you. This is my blood of the covenant, which is poured out for many for the forgiveness of sins'."* (Matthew 26:26-28)

I. In between the bread and chalice on the table is the letter "A," which Ed placed there to represent the Alpha, the first letter of the Greek alphabet. "It was the beginning of the alphabet" Ed explains, "the beginning of our Christianity or the thought pattern, and there is no ending to his government, so I only display the alpha." He did not place the omega there, which is the last letter of the Greek alphabet. In the Old Testament, God says He is the first and the last: *"Who has done such mighty deeds, summoning each new generation from the beginning of time? It is I, the LORD, the First and the Last. I alone am he."* (Isaiah 41:4 NLV). Jesus refers to himself as the Alpha and the Omega several times in Revelations: *"'I am the Alpha and the Omega,' says the Lord God, who is and was*

and is to come--the Almighty." (Revelation 1:8); *"When I saw Him, I fell at His feet like a dead man. But He placed His right hand on me and said, 'Do not be afraid. I am the First and the Last'."* (Revelation 1:17); *"I am the Alpha and the Omega, the First and the Last, the Beginning and the End."* (Revelation 22:13)

J. On the table cloth below the A is a musical scale Ed calls the sound of the universe, the song without words.

K. Beneath the table are Jesus's feet, which Ed left exposed to represent the washing of the feet. *"The evening meal was in progress, and the devil had already prompted Judas, the son of Simon Iscariot, to betray Jesus. Jesus knew that the Father had put all things under his power, and that he had come from God and was returning to God; so he got up from the meal, took off his outer clothing, and wrapped a towel around his waist. After that, he poured water into a basin and began to wash his disciples' feet, drying them with the towel that was wrapped around him."* (John 13:2-5). Jesus washed his apostles' feet to show he came to earth as a servant. *"For even the Son of Man came not to be served but to serve others and to give his life as a ransom for many."* (Matthew 20:28)

L. The shape at the very bottom of the panel is there to show perspective that Jesus is sitting.

PANEL FIVE

A The first symbol at the top of the panel is the very faint word "Irod." Irod is the Romanian translation for Herod, as shown in the scripture from Luke 23:6-8 on Biblica.com: *"6 Când a auzit acest lucru, Pilat a întrebat dacă Omul este galileean 7 și, aflând că este sub autoritatea lui Irod, L-a trimis la* **Irod**, *care se afla și el în Ierusalim în zilele acelea. 8* **Irod** *s-a bucurat foarte mult când L-a văzut pe Isus, pentru că de multă vreme dorea să-L vadă, din pricina a ceea ce auzise despre El, și spera să-L vadă înfăptuind vreun semn."*[21] The same scripture in English reads, *6 "Oh, is he a Galilean?" Pilate asked. 7 When they said that he*

21 "Luca 23 - Nouă Traducere În Limba Română (NTLR)," Biblica, accessed January 4, 2017, https://www.biblica.com/bible/ntlr/luca/23/.

was, Pilate sent him to Herod Antipas, because Galilee was under Herod's jurisdiction, and Herod happened to be in Jerusalem at the time. 8 Herod was delighted at the opportunity to see Jesus, because he had heard about him and had been hoping for a long time to see him perform a miracle."[22]

It was Herod's court that Jesus was sent to prior to his crucifixion, and Herod who beheaded the Apostle James the Greater.

B. Above the word Irod is the word ZWN, which is the Greek word for "Life." The Hebrew meaning of the name Eve is also "Life." The Greek spelling for the word "Life" is ZWN (ζωή). Ed placed the word ZWN there to represent Eve.

C. Above the word ZWN is the faint shape of perhaps a star or perhaps a cross. Does it represent the north star or Jesus on the cross? When asked, Ed would always say, "You decide."

D. Next to the star is the second faint image of a cherub, one of two that appear on either side of Jesus. Ed says this image also represents the female servers, present but not talked about, at the last supper.

E. JAMES THE GREATER: The first apostle depicted on this panel is James, also known as James the Greater or James the Elder. He was the brother of the Apostle John and was fishing with him and their father when Jesus asked them to put down their nets and follow him. James was the only apostle whose death was mentioned in the New Testament and so he is thought to be the first of the apostles to be martyred.

F. Herod beheaded James for his teachings, and the sword shown on the table is his martyr symbol.

G. The three shells next to the sword are also symbolic of his pilgrimage by sea.

H. There are also four hidden heart symbols: one on James's right chest area (when looking straight at him), and the other three on

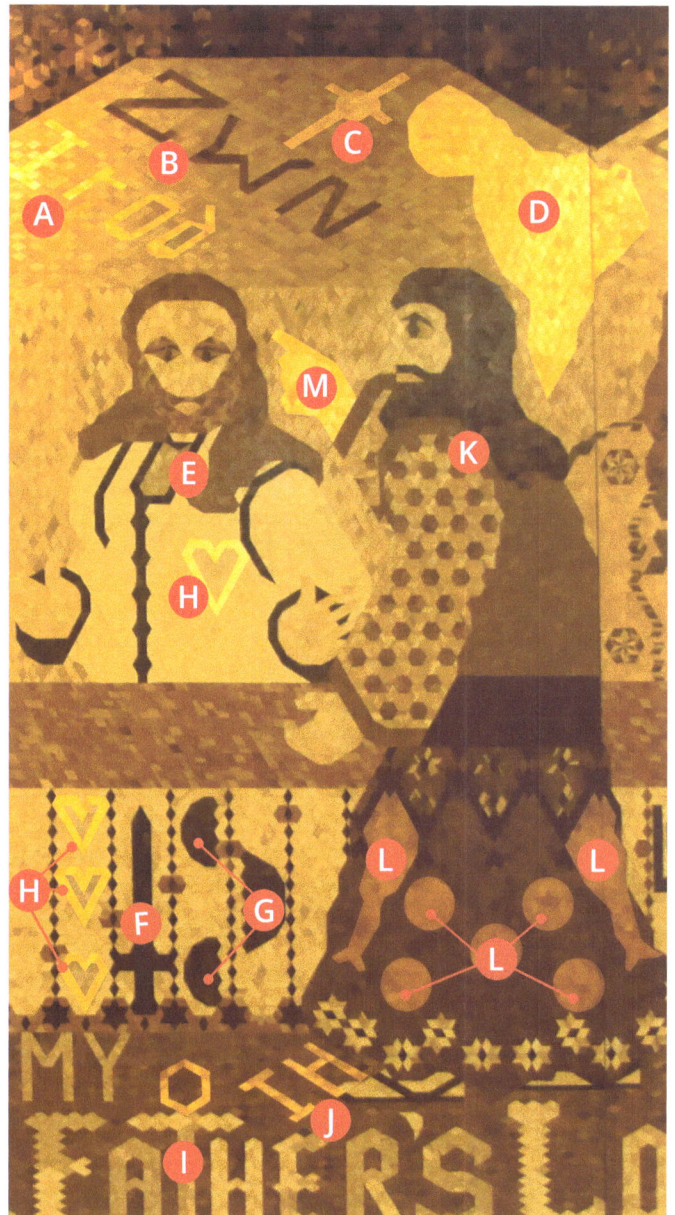

the table, vertical within the musical scale on the tablecloth.

I. Below the table is the name of the panel, *My Father's Love*. Above the T in the word Faher's" is a circle or head, thought to represent Christ on the cross. It also looks rather like the female gender symbol ♀.

J. To the right of the T are two diagonal letters, IH, and the beginning of another letter just visible under the garment. The letters IHS are a Christogram, which is a monogram for the name of Jesus. The Greek spelling of Jesus is IHΣΥΣ, with the first three letters translated as IHS, often used to represent him[23].

---

22 "Luke 23 - New Living Translation (NLT)," Biblica, , accessed January 4, 2017, https://www.biblica.com/bible/nlt/luke/23/.

23 "Christogram," New World Encyclopedia, accessed January 12, 2017, http://www.newworldencyclopedia.org/p/index.

K. PHILIP: The apostle next to James is Philip, the one to whom Jesus first said, "Follow me," and who told Bartholomew that the one Moses and the prophets wrote about was found.

L. Philip is most known as the one whom Jesus asked where they could buy enough bread to feed 5,000 people. On the bottom of Philip's garment, very dark and hard to see, is his symbol: two fish, one on each side, and five circles representing loaves of bread.

M. Philip is pointing to the word Irod as if he knows that it was Irod who killed James the Greater.

PANEL SIX

A. The first word across the top of this panel is "LOGOS," spelled λόγος in Greek. The primary meaning of Logos is "word." In the New Testament, John describes Jesus as the Logos (the word) when he says, *"In the beginning was the Word, and the Word was with God, and the Word was God (Ἐν ἀρχῇ ἦν ὁ **λόγος**, καὶ ὁ **λόγος** ἦν πρὸς τὸν θεόν, καὶ θεὸς ἦν ὁ **λόγος**)"*[24] John 1:1.

B. Next to LOGOS, very faint, is "WORD." Ed, again, is referring to Jesus as the Word of God.

C. Next to "WORD" is the Greek word for "Savior." The Greeks spelled it several ways, including: σωτήρ, Σωτήρας or Σωτήρ [25]. In John 4:42, many Samaritans professed to believe that Jesus is the savior of the world: *"They said to the woman, 'We no longer believe just because of what you said; now we have heard for ourselves, and we know that this man really is the Savior of the world'."* The Greek version of this scripture reads, *"τῇ τε γυναικὶ ἔλεγον ὅτι Οὐκέτι διὰ τὴν σὴν λαλιὰν πιστεύομεν· αὐτοὶ γὰρ ἀκηκόαμεν, καὶ οἴδαμεν ὅτι οὗτός ἐστιν ἀληθῶς ὁ **Σωτὴρ** τοῦ κόσμου."*[26]

php?tile=Christogram&oldid=969357.

24 "John 1:1 Greek Text Analysis," BibleHub, , accessed January 10, 2017, http://biblehub.com/text/john/1-1.htm.

25 "Savior," Google Translate, accessed December 29, 2016, https://translate.google.com/?um=1&ie=UTF-8&hl=en&client=tw-ob#en/el/Savior.

26 "John 4:42 Greek Text Analysis," BibleHub, accessed December 29, 2016, http://biblehub.com/text/john/4-42.htm.

D. SIMON THE ZEALOT: The first person pictured on the left is Simon the Zealot, or the other Simon. The Zealots were a fanatical group that rebelled against the Roman Empire, but Simon left the Zealots to follow Jesus.[27] Ed learned that Simon left for India right after the crucifixion to teach about the risen Christ, so he dressed Simon in Indian garb, which is the thought pattern Ed embraced while assembling him.

E. On Simon's garb are four circles that Ed calls prayer wheels. Research finds that a prayer wheel is a medieval wheel that "consists of six concentric circles containing quotes from the Lord's Prayer, the Beatitudes, the book of Isaiah and incidents from the life of Jesus. At its center is the Latin word for 'God.'"[28] Ed also says the four circles could represent the four corners of the earth, or the symbols for air, water, fire and earth.

F. Simon's symbol is the Bible because he preached the Gospel. Ed displayed Simon's Bible on the table encasing the word, "Holy."

G. Below Simon's symbol is a towel with the words "I AM" on it draped over a footstool. I AM is the name God told Moses to give to the Israelites if they asked who sent him. "*Moses said to God, 'Suppose I go to the Israelites and say to them, 'The God of your fathers has sent me to you,' and they ask me, 'What is his name?' Then what shall I tell them?' God said to Moses, 'I AM WHO I AM. This is what you are to say to the Israelites: 'I AM has sent me to you.' God also said to Moses, 'Say to the Israelites, 'The LORD, the God of your fathers—the God of Abraham, the God of Isaac and the God of Jacob—has sent me to you.' 'This is my name forever, the name you shall call me from generation to generation.'"* (Exodus 3:13-15)

The stool is where Jesus sat to wash the Apostles' feet and then dried them with the towel of the Great I AM. It was tradition to wash your feet before a communal meal. He also did it to cleanse them in his salvation, and to give them an example of what they are to do for others.

H. At the bottom of the stool is ΘΕΟΥ (Θεός), a Greek word for God. These letters translated from the Greek New Testament to English become Theos, also meaning God.

I. JAMES THE LESSER: Next to Simon is James, also known as James the Lesser because he is younger than James the Greater.

J. When James the Lesser was martyred, his body was cut in half and into pieces with a saw. Note the handsaw, which Ed designed into his belt.

K. Hanging from his belt is a light or lantern, signifying that Jesus is the light of the world. Inside the lantern are the other two square pieces Ed placed in honor of his own father who taught him the craft of marquetry.

L. Above James's belt is the Hebrew letter that looks like a W (ש), called the shin. The Hebrew meaning for the word shin is "tooth" or "sharp."[29] Ed also placed it there to signify ownership. In Rabbinic Hebrew, the letters של spell "SHEL," which means possession or ownership.[30] Ed claims the letter denotes the ownership we have in the church today, at the end of the pews or at the pulpit. Ed claims the letter has nothing to do with James, but he wanted to include the concept in a non-intrusive way, so he chose to place it there.

M. At the bottom of James's garment is the basin Jesus used to wash his disciples' feet. The water was sacred, and its color is dark red symbolizing blood. The Twelve Apostles were baptized in the blood of the Great I AM when Jesus washed their feet.

N. Very faintly placed on the basin is the year 1986, the year Ed finished this panel series.

27 "Who were the 12 disciples?" Bibleinfo.com, accessed January 6, 2017, http://www.bibleinfo.com/en/questions/who-were-twelve-disciples#simon-zealot.

28 David Van Biema, "How readers 'solved' the mystery of the prayer wheel," Religion News Service, July 07, 2016, accessed January 10, 2017, http://religionnews.com/2015/05/15/readers-solved-mystery-prayer-wheel/.

29 Jeff A. Benner, "The Ancient Hebrew Alphabet - Shin," Ancient-Hebrew.org, , accessed January 11, 2017, http://www.ancient-hebrew.org/alphabet_letters_shin.html.

30 "SHEL – Who Does this belong to?" My Hebrew Word, April 27, 2014, accessed January 11, 2017, https://myhebrewwords.wordpress.com/2014/04/27/5-%D7%A9%D7%9C-shel-who-does-this-belong-to/.

Ed says this was his second beginning; the time when he began his second life.

PANEL SEVEN

A. On the top left of the seventh panel is "BE-HOLD OUR KING." Ed explains Jesus is not just the Jewish king, he is our king. Ed says, "He is my king, or our king; I will share him."

B. The letter "g" in "KING" looks like the number 9, which in Christian symbolism, means completion. Ed also used the number 9 in place of the letter "g" on panels where Jesus is being crucified on the cross.

C. THADDEUS: The next apostle is Thaddeus. He was also known as Lebbeus, Jude, or the other Judas, and was brother to James the Lesser. Roman Catholics know him as Saint Jude, the saint of lost or desperate causes.[31]

D. In the center of his garment, Ed placed numerous symbols that could have many meanings. We see several triangles which are symbolic in many cultures. In Christianity, the triangle is the symbol for the Trinity—Father, Son, and Holy Ghost. Two triangles interlaced, creating a six-pointed star, is the symbol for the Star of David (also Shield of David or Magen David) in Judaism. The triangle placed with the point down is a symbol for female, and the triangle placed with the point up is the symbol for male.[32]

There are two shapes that look like crescent moons, or possibly an eclipse. It is said, "The eclipse of the Sun would represent the fall of Adam and God's grace solution, the substitutionary death of the Lord Jesus Christ on the Cross to provide redemption. Just as the first Adam died in an eclipse, the second Adam would die in an eclipse. After the eclipse, there would be light from the Sun again, which represents the Resurrection."[33]

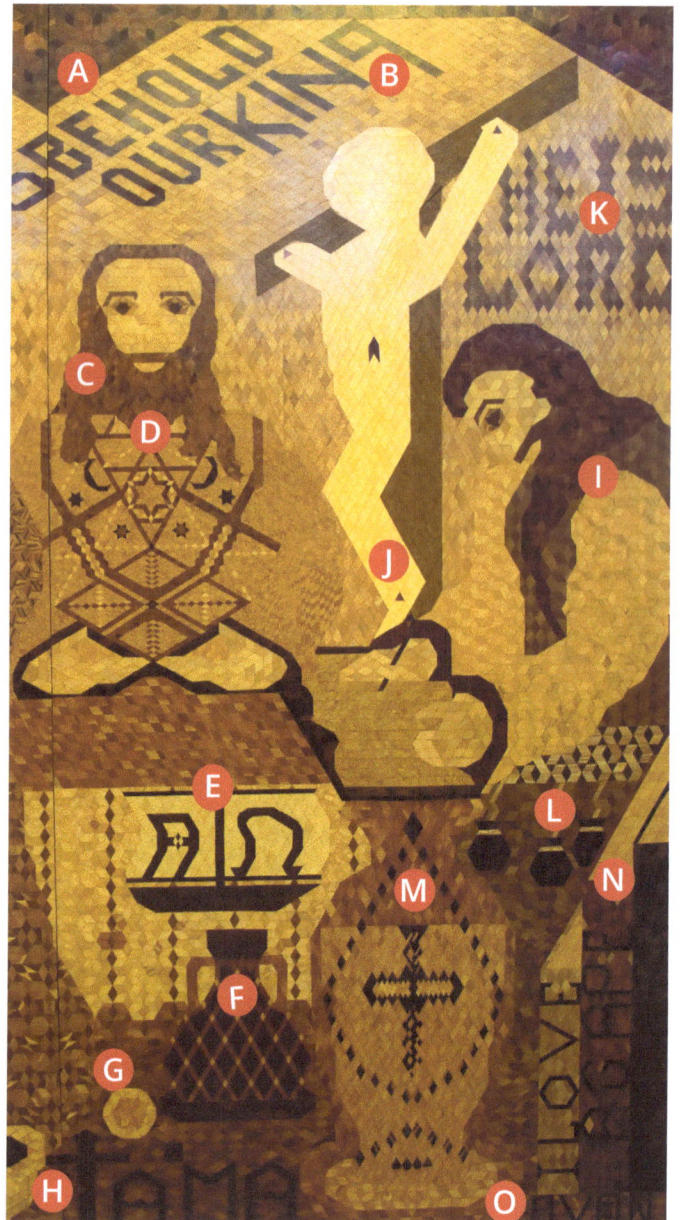

There are also four small six-pointed stars, or hexagons placed here. "In Christianity, the hexagram is the Creator's Star or Star of Creation. Its six points stand for the six days of creation, and also represent the six attributes of God: power, wisdom, majesty, love, mercy and justice."[34]

The fact that there are four stars placed here could have numerous meanings. The number four has several symbolic meanings, including the four Gospels, the four corners of the earth, the four winds of Heaven, and the four guardians of the throne of God, to name just a few. It also looks like Thaddeus is hold-

31 "Who were the 12 disciples?" Bibleinfo.com, accessed January 6, 2017, http://www.bibleinfo.com/en/questions/who-were-twelve-disciples#jude-thaddeus.

32 "The Triangle," The State of Symbols, accessed January 12, 2017, http://thestateofsymbols.com/the-triangle/.

33 Larry Wood, "Lunar Eclipse," Bible Doctrine News, accessed January 12, 2017, http://www.biblenews1.com/history0/20000120eclipse.htm.

34 "Six-Point Star (Hexagram; Star of David)," ReligionFacts, January 19, 2017, accessed January 12, 2017, http://www.religionfacts.com/six-point-star.

ing four blocks, again having numerous possible meanings, including the heavenly city of God shaped as a perfect square, a solid foundation, or the four elements of fire, water, air and earth.[35]

E. There is much debate over Thaddeus's name, his symbol, and how he died. One symbol for Thaddeus is the ship, representing the many missions he went on preaching the gospel. Ed placed his symbol of a ship on the table, and explains that the wind can distort the story. "No matter how careful you are, you find variance as you read the different versions. There is a distortion someplace, but not enough to cause any harm."

Ed placed the symbols of Alpha and Omega, one on each sail, to represent the beginning and the end, but Ed knew that history and eternity could be distorted by the wind or the voice of individuals. The symbol of the ship is also there to represent how Ed believed Thaddeus was martyred. According to Ed, Thaddeus was keelhauled: tied with a rope by the wrists and legs and dragged beneath a sailboat to be torn apart by the barnacles. Then, they simply cut the ropes and left him to feed the fish.

F. Under the symbol of the ship is a wine cask from which Jesus poured the wine and from which he had the apostles drink, symbolizing his blood; *"This is my blood of the everlasting covenant, which is poured for many."* (Mark 14:24).

G. On the bottom left side of the wine cask is a light circle which Ed says is a crumb that fell from the table for the dogs like him. In Matthew 15:26-28, the Canaanite woman expressed her faith to Jesus, *"But Jesus replied, 'it is not right to take the children's bread and toss it to the dogs.' 'Yes, Lord', she said, 'even the dogs eat the crumbs that fall from their master's table.'"* Ed says, "No matter how I have lived, my Father said I was entitled. Even as a dog, I am entitled to share the Lord's Supper. You can't bar me from that."

H. Under the crumb is the word "TAMA," a Greek word meaning vow or promise.[36] Ed explains that at the time of Christ, the TAMA was a person's testimony, something he wrote and signed and no one could change. Ed claims this work to be his TAMA.

I. MATTHEW: The last apostle in the series is Matthew, also called Levi. He was a tax collector, despised by the Jews, yet chosen by Jesus to follow him. Unlike the other apostles, Matthew could write, and wrote one of the four Gospels.[37] Ed displays him writing about Christ and the crucifixion.

J. An image of the crucifixion is coming out of Matthew's pen as he writes about it. The points of blood in the hands, the side, and the feet are present.

K. Above Matthew's head is the phrase, HE IS LORD. Ed explains that the Anglo-Saxon translation comes from the Old Testament. In the beginning was Jehovah, the Great God, the single God who created the multiple. Ed explains that when the Bible transitions into claiming "Lord God," it is referring to the promise of the Messiah, the Son of God, the Lord God, Jesus.

L. Beneath Matthew are three money bags, his symbol as a tax collector.

M. To the left of the money bags is a water cask that held the water Jesus used to wash the Apostles' feet.

N. Below the money bags are three books titled *I LOVE*, *AGAPE*, and *FATHER*. These are the three books Ed read that helped him learn and come to his conclusions. Ed says if you read them differently, they say, "I LOVE A GREAT APE," symbolizing the theory of evolution. He said it's your choice, you can either love the agape father, which is love itself, or you can love a great ape. When talking about the book *Agape*, Ed may be talking about the book written by the theologian Anders Nygren called,

35 Tenzin Gyurme, The Sacred Numerology of ThoTh, Lulu Press, Inc, 2013, accessed January 21, 2018, https://books.google.com/books?id=cV9RCwAAQBAJ&printsec=frontcover#v=onepage&q&f=false.

36 Linda Theodorou, "T is for Tamata," Churches in Greece, January 01, 1970, accessed January 12, 2017, http://churchesingreece.blogspot.com/2014/01/t-is-for-tamata.html.

37 "Who were the 12 disciples?" Bibleinfo.com, accessed January 6, 2017, http://www.bibleinfo.com/en/questions/who-were-twelve-disciples#matthew-levi.

Agape and Eros. In the book, Nygren explains that agape is the highest form of love, not sexual or romantic, but brotherly and spiritual.[38]

O. Under the three books is the name Avon. Avon is a symbol for Ed's first born daughter, Jean Evon. Instead of E, Ed used A in Avon to represent the first (alpha) for first born.

---

38 Thomas Jay Oord, "Agape Theology," For The Love of Wisdom and The Wisdom of Love, December 28, 2016, accessed October 13, 2016, http://thomasjayoord.com/index.php/blog/archives/agape_theology.

Simon and the Lamb

This panel series is called *Simon and The Lamb* and it depicts the scene in the Bible when Simon of Cyrene was seized by the Romans to carry the cross for a severely beaten Jesus as he traveled the road to Calvary to be crucified. Scripture says, *"As the soldiers led him away, they seized Simon from Cyrene, who was on his way in from the country, and put the cross on him and made him carry it behind Jesus."* Luke 23:26.

Ed explains that this panel series symbolizes his life and what his job is all about. He believed that pain is the greatest teacher for man and woman, and when man is hurt to the point that he can no longer stand, he is basically a dead man walking. That is when the Father creates someone to carry his cross for just a moment so he can take a breath and stand up again to take his burdens back on his shoulders. Ed believed he had many Simons in his own life who carried his own cross for him until he recovered and could take it back. They didn't need the punishment or the pain, but they carried it just for him.

While pain is the greatest teacher, Ed believed love comes in afterward and smooths out the pain so that it becomes understandable. When Ed thinks about the love of the Great Energy, and of his family, it gives him a moment of softness and gives him the desire to go on with his job. He also describes the female enduring immense pain when going through childbirth. She knows what she is about to experience, but does it anyway out of love for the male and love for the child. It is her job to have children who will eventually take over the father's job when he dies. Ed explains that each one of us experiences a level of pain, but we are not all tried beyond our own abilities to withstand it and learn by it. When pain brings us to our knees, we call out to the Father to take it away, and He replaces the pain with pure love. Pure love is usually considered a female thing, but men have it too. They borrow it or get it from their mothers or grandmothers or some other female. They typically do not get it from their own kind.

A. The first person on the left is a Roman soldier and he is carrying the ensign for the Holy Roman Empire. An ensign is a symbol for a tribe or army that sits on top of a pole and is carried by a soldier at the front of the army as they march into battle. The eagle, also called the aquila, is the ensign for the Holy Roman Empire.[39]

B. Next is Simon of Cyrene carrying the cross for Jesus. Cyrene is located on the coast of Africa, now known as Libya. Many Jews lived there and traveled over 900 miles to Jerusalem for Passover, and it is believed that Simon was one of them.[40] Because Jesus was beaten so badly and struggled to carry the heavy cross, Roman soldiers saw Simon in the crowd and "compelled" him to pick it up and carry it for him. It is also thought that after this experience, Simon went back to Cyrene a believer in Christ and his two sons, Alexander and Rufus, became active in the Christian movement and were even mentioned in the gospel of Mark, *"And they compel one Simon a Cyrenian, who passed by, coming out of the country, the father of Alexander and Rufus, to*

bear his cross." (Mark 15:21).

C. On the cross are several words written in various languages. Ultimately, Ed wants to demonstrate seven languages in the geometrics of their original form on the post and crossbeam. He chose these particular words because he could construct them in 60-degree angles and illustrate them at various points. Ed claims that if you look at the cross from various angles and in different lighting, you will see different words. Along the shaft of the cross, Ed wrote the word "Savior" in Hebrew: עִישׁומ or לְאוֹג. Can you see it? He says that Simon was Jesus's savior just for a moment when he helped him carry the cross.

On the crossbeam, there are several words that are hard to see. Ed claimed he wrote, "Jehovah is not my punisher," in ancient Babylonian. He also wrote EL, which is the oldest name for God[41], and it also happens to be Ed's initials. Finally, he wrote the word God in Hebrew: םיהולא and in Greek: Θεός. Can you see it?

Ed pointed out, if he did it correctly, the word "Pain" is on one end of the cross member and balanced out exactly on the other end is the word "Love." Can you see it?

According to Ed, the upright post and cross member is the strongest formation there is, and the building block of everything. It also represents the strongest member of humanity, the female. When man is feeling uncomfortable with pain, she balances it with love, being careful not to over-love, but loving just enough for him to get up and continue his job.

D. When you look at Simon's face, it changes color as you view it from one side to the other. Looking at it straight on, his face is dark and his nose is lighter. As you move to the left, his face becomes lighter and his nose becomes darker.

E. In front of Simon, on his knees and in shackles, is Jesus. He is brought to his knees from the pain he is enduring as he is scourged in

39 "Roman Standard," Tribunes and Triumphs, accessed January 10, 2017, http://www.tribunesandtriumphs.org/roman-army/roman-standard.htm.
40 Richard J. Grebenc, "Carrying the Cross with Simon of Cyrene," Homiletic & Pastoral Review, April 13, 2014, accessed July 9, 2017, http://www.hprweb.com/2014/04/carrying-the-cross-with-simon-of-cyrene/.
41 "The Hebrew Names for God - El," Hebrew for Christians, accessed July 8, 2017, http://www.hebrew4christians.com/Names_of_G-d/El/el.html.

front of the people who rejected him. They spit on him and throw stones at him as he is brutally whipped and tortured before being sentenced to crucifixion.

F. On Jesus's back are the bloody wounds, or stripes, caused by the beating. You can see the shape of the Rabbinic Hebrew letter ש on his back called the Shin and it indicates ownership or possession. Ed says it is a logo signifying that Rome has taken ownership of him and they have the authority to crucify him.

G. Ed designed Jesus wearing an American Indian headband because he says he relates to the concept of the Indian. Ed studied Native Americans and their beliefs, and much of the meanings and symbols throughout the panels represent his interpretations from this knowledge.

H. Jesus is wearing a white garment, signifying purity and holiness.

I. Above Jesus is the accuser. He is pointing at Jesus and accusing him of being a false prophet. He is also wearing white because he perceives himself as being holy.

J. The soldier to the right of Jesus is holding up three spikes in one hand and has a hammer in the other hand. He is ready and impatiently waiting to nail Jesus to the cross.

K. To the left of Jesus is the punisher, whipping and scourging him with the cat-o'-nine-tails. This is a brutal weapon consisting of at least three long strands of leather with sharp pieces of bone on the ends and weighted with balls made of lead. This weapon isn't designed to just cause bruising; it is designed to lacerate the skin, the veins, and arteries, causing unimaginable pain to the point of near death.[42]

L. On the top of the panel, it reads: "This Is His Son" signifying that Jesus is the Son of God.

M. On the bottom is the name for this panel series, *Simon and The Lamb*.

Ed used various woods with several shades of colors to help tell this story. You can see the green of sumac, symbolizing perfection. Cherry wood is used for the soldier with the cat-o'-nine-tails to indicate love for the whip. Mahogany is used to symbolize the softness of love itself. The cross is made from thorn apple to represent the law, the thorn in our sides, and heartfelt pain.

42 David McClister, "The Scourging of Jesus," Truth Magazine Online - Conservative Christian Bible Study Materials, accessed July 16, 2017, http://www.truthmagazine.com/archives/volume44/v440106010.htm.

RAISING OF CHRIST

This panel series is called *Raising of Christ* and is the first in a trilogy of panels depicting the crucifixion of Jesus. It displays the moments after Roman soldiers pounded nails into the hands of Jesus and raised him up on the cross.

Ed says that this panel series is a representation of his own concept of love. He already explained *My Father's Love* and *My Mother's Love*. This series is Ed's perception and feelings about love. He starts out with the raising of Christ, the Messiah, who is the combination of the Great Energy, male and female, and the product of their love.

Ed explains that, when he was younger, they used to build fences by digging holes in the ground and lifting tall posts with a board. They put a rope around the post while a horse or team of men pulled the post up and dropped it into the hole, landing on a rock. Ed surmises that this is the way the crucifixion took place—they nailed Jesus to the cross member on the ground, they raised the post into the air with a board and a rope, then the cross dropped into a hole in the ground with a jolt—the first jolt of the crucifixion.

A. At the bottom of the first panel is the name of this series, *Raising of Christ*.

B. Just above the name are three soldiers gambling over who would own the royal purple robe that was placed on Jesus, along with the crown of thorns, to taunt him, calling him, "King of the Jews." When they finished mocking him, they took the robe off and put his own garments back on and led him away. *"Pilate answered, 'What I have written, I have written.' When the soldiers had crucified Jesus, they divided His garments into four parts, one for each soldier, with the tunic remaining. It was seamless, woven in one piece from the top to bottom. So they said to one another, 'Let's not tear it, but instead let us cast lots to see who will get it.' This was to fulfill the Scripture: 'They divided My garments among them, and cast lots for My clothing.' So that is what the soldiers did."* (John 19-23)

Ed explains that, when they cast lots, they gathered around the circle and put their name or symbol into a hat or container of some kind. They walked around the circle and pulled a name out, and whoever was the winner of the lottery won whatever they were gambling for.

C. To represent casting lots, Ed decided to use a more modern concept of using playing cards or dice. The person to the right is either holding two cards or two dice. As dice, they each look the same, but if you measure them, they are different sizes to signify the term "crooked dice" or "loaded dice"—where the dice are weighted on one end so that they land on the lower number and the person loses.[43] Ed also designed the dice with "snake eyes"—each dice has one pip, meaning each has a value of one, the lowest roll possible. When you put the pair together they look like snake eyes.[44]

D. Each of the players also represents a deck of cards. The player on the right is the Jack of Diamonds, and you can see diamonds on his arm cuffs and his belt. The player in the center holding the robe is the King of Clubs (although you cannot see his belt). The player on the left is the Queen of Hearts, representing that the female was present, and she has hearts on her arm cuffs and belt. The person standing behind the Queen of Hearts is the King of Spades, with spades on his belt.

E. The King of Spades is holding a sign with Ed's signature on it: 6-22-34. The number 6 on the sign is backward, which Ed placed to symbolize that, at that moment, two time-periods are being straddled—we are moving from one period of time, or coming from behind, to the next period of time, or the eternity to come.

F. To the right of the King of Spades is John leading Mary, mother of Jesus, away as they both weep, John with a tear in his eyes. Scripture says, *"Now there stood by the cross of Jesus His mother, and His mother's sister, Mary the wife of Clopas, and Mary Magdalene. When Jesus therefore saw His mother, and the disciple whom He loved standing by, He said to His mother, 'Woman,*

behold your son!' Then He said to the disciple, 'Behold your mother!' And from that hour that disciple took her to his own home." (John 19:25-9)

G. To the bottom right of Mary is the date 1998, the year Ed completed this panel.

H. At the bottom of the second panel, we see the accuser pointing his finger at Jesus as he is lifted on the cross. He is shouting, "Crucify him! Crucify him!"

I. To the right of the accuser is the soldier holding the hammer that drove the nails into the feet of Jesus.

J   Surrounding the cross are several men helping to raise Jesus. Ed says he placed himself in the panel as one of the men that helped crucify Jesus, but he doesn't specify which one he is. You decide.

K. In the center, Jesus is nailed to the cross. Ed explains that his hands, arms, and legs were the most difficult parts to design out of all of the panels because of the various angles involved. "To get the angle of the cross, the angle of the Christ, the arms and hands, the rope, and so on, all at the right places...to get the numbers right and the colors right—that was a bummer," Ed says. "You should try that some day on a piece of paper."

L. Jesus is dressed in his working garment, which Ed explains is like a towel. Men wore this white garment around their waists to keep their privates covered. When it was time to work, they pulled the garment between their legs and tucked one end of it into the top of the wrap to secure it. According to Ed, Jesus is ready to work here.

M. Jesus is wearing a crown of thorns on his head. The crown is made of the green wood, sumac, which Ed retrieved from the forty acres he once owned. If you shine a black light on it, the crown actually glows in the dark. Note here also that the eyes of Jesus are peaceful, symbolizing He is at peace with his purpose of dying for us.

N. On the third panel, we see three women including Mary Magdalene, Mary of Clapas, the

43 "Loaded Dice," Wordnik.com, , accessed September 3, 2017, https://www.wordnik.com/words/loaded%20dice.
44 S"Snake Eyes," Wolfram MathWorld, , accessed September 3, 2017, http://mathworld.wolfram.com/SnakeEyes.html.

sister of the mother Mary, and Salome, who stayed by Christ through his crucifixion. Ed says these women represent all females because it was their gift to the world that was crucified. They remained at the foot of the cross, they embalmed Jesus after he was brought down from the cross, and they announced the resurrection. While the Apostles chose to hide, glimpsing at the crucifixion from a distance, the women remained present, steadfast and loyal.

O. Below the three women is a man with a post helping to drop the cross into the hole and another man on a horse pulling the rope to help lift the cross up and into place.

Ed explains that men have a very difficult time understanding the crucifixion because they don't fully understand female love and how deep it is.

DADDY

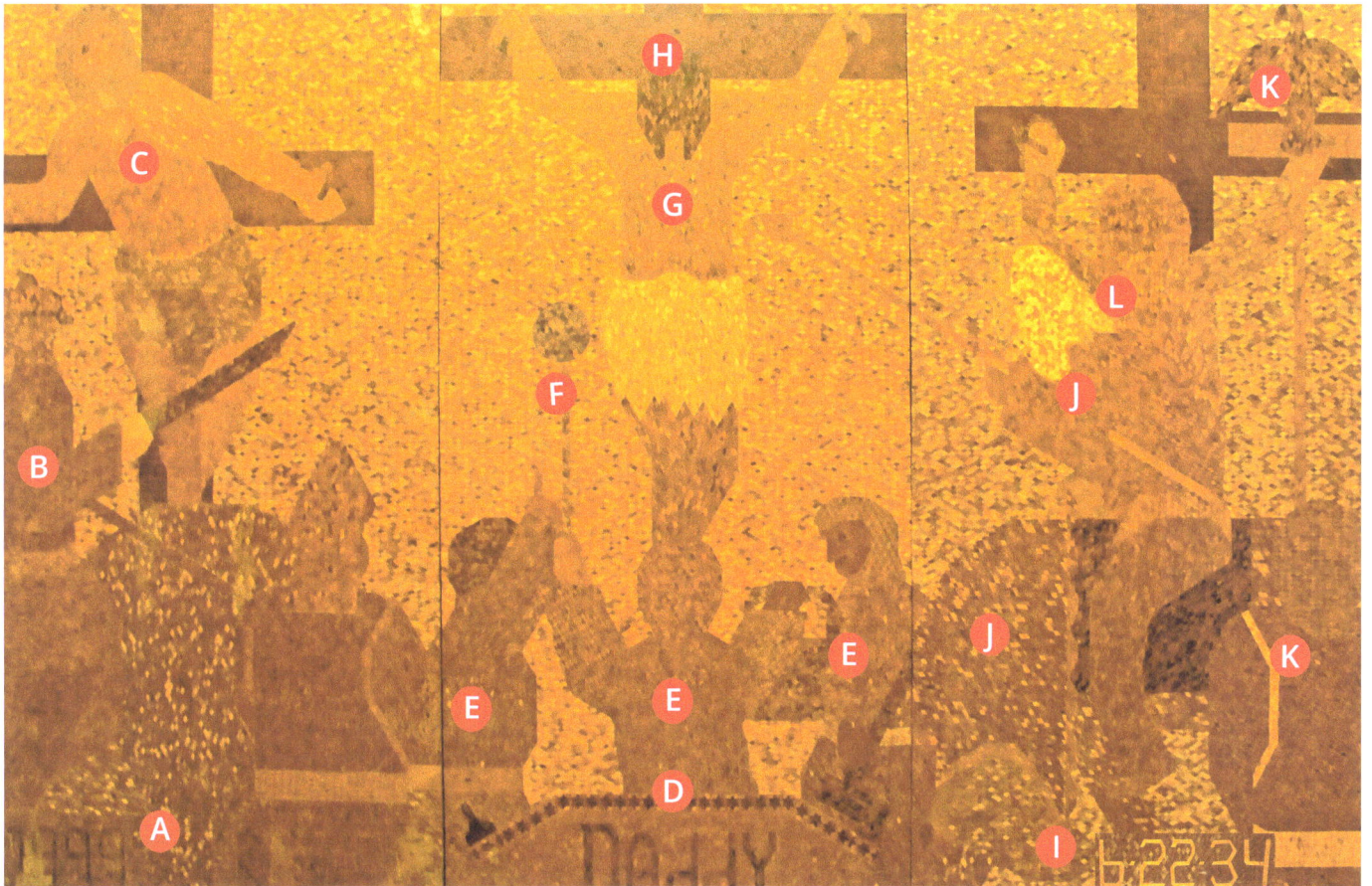

The name of this panel series is *Daddy* because, as Ed explains the naming of it, this is the moment that God became Ed's daddy and Ed himself was adopted into God's family.

The crucifixion represents a changing of the times, a phenomenon that started in the Garden of Eden. Ed says that the *AdamEve* panel and this panel are similar in meaning, in that this panel also represents the changing of the times. God caused Adam to fall into a deep sleep so that He could take one of Adam's ribs to create woman: the first changing of time. Later, God banished Adam and Eve from the Garden of Eden for eating the forbidden fruit: another changing of the times.

Here, Christ has died and the piercing of his side marks another changing of the times.

The son of the Great Energy has died—love is dead. Ed explains that now you have the stopping of one time and the beginning of another. The Christian era starts with the ceasing of the law that required blood sacrifices because Jesus

shed his blood for us all. In the Old Testament, there was no love involved, just law being expressed for thousands of years. When Jesus was born and walked the earth as a man, he taught about God's love. He freed us from the punishment of death because he loved us. Ed wants us to remember that Jesus's life wasn't taken from him, rather Jesus laid it down willingly. The penalty for the sins of Adam and Eve in the Garden of Eden have been paid, and the judgment is over. The answer that all men have been searching for is love. Jesus said, *"A new command I give you: Love one another. As I have loved you, so you must love one another. By this all men will know that you are my disciples, if you love one another."* (John 13:34-35); *"There is a saying, 'Love your friends and hate your enemies.' But I say: Love your enemies! Pray for those who persecute you! In that way you will be acting as true sons of your Father in heaven. For he gives his sunlight to both the evil and the good, and sends rain on the just and on the unjust too. If you love only those who love you, what good is that? Even scoundrels do that much. If you are friendly only to your friends, how are you different from anyone else? Even the heathen do that. But you are to be perfect, even as your Father in heaven is perfect."* (Matthew 5:43-48)

A. When looking at the panel series from left to right, notice at the bottom of the first panel is the year Ed completed this panel: 1999.

B. Above the year is a Centurion holding a sword while seated on a horse, and there is another soldier standing to his right.

C. Above them, hanging on a cross, is one of the thieves crucified at the same time as Jesus. He is the thief that rebuked the other thief for insulting Jesus. He asked Jesus to remember him in the kingdom, and Jesus told him he would be with him in paradise. Notice he is raised up on the cross because, Ed explains, he will rise up to heaven.

D. At the bottom of the center panel is the name of the series, *Daddy*.

E. Above the name are three people dancing around the cross. Ed explains that this dancing symbolizes dancing around the maypole. When Ed was a child, people would dance with orange and green ribbons around a pole to celebrate the coming of spring, a ritual often practiced in European countries.[45] Spring brings about rebirth, when plants and animals awaken and blossom. Ed believed that Jesus is spring, the cross is the maypole, and the dancers are celebrating the arrival of spring with life itself, the rebirth of creation.

F. The dancer in the center is raising a long pole with a ball on the end up into the air, symbolizing new life from old. The dancer to the right is holding a basket that has old fruit and new fruit, also symbolizing new life.

   According to Ed, the person on the left is the accuser pointing at Jesus. The person in the center is holding up a stick with a sponge on it to wet the lips of Jesus when he proclaimed, "I thirst." The person on the right is holding a pail with fermented vinegar in it used to wet the sponge. *"After this, Jesus knowing that all things were now accomplished, that the scripture might be fulfilled, saith, I thirst. Now there was set a vessel full of vinegar: and they filled a spunge with vinegar, and put it upon hyssop, and put it to his mouth."* (John 19:28-29)

G. Above the dancers is Jesus, dead on the cross. He proclaimed, "It is finished," and then hung his head in death as he bore the sins of the world.

H. Jesus's head is just below the cross member, which has a symbolic meaning. Ed explains that the joining of the cross beam and post is the strongest building material in the world. With Jesus's head just below the cross member, we are taken back to the Garden of Eden and the first Adam, the first story. If you build on top of the cross member, the strong foundation for the second story, this is where we are now. After the death of Jesus, he became the second story, the second Adam. Ed also explains that it is like the mark of Cain, the protection God put on Cain so that he would not be murdered by others.[46] The cross is our protection.

I. Ed's signature is at the bottom right: 6-22-34.

J. Above the signature is a soldier on a horse holding the spear that pierced the side of Jesus to prove he was dead. The soldier has no face, signifying that he could be any of us. The horse is bowing in recognition that Jesus is the Messiah and became the blood sacrifice for all.

K. To the right of the horse is a Roman soldier holding the ensign of the Roman empire, the eagle. Normally, the eagle's wings would be spanned out as if in flight. Ed purposely designed this eagle with dropped wings because it cowered before the king.

L. Above the soldier with the spear is the other thief crucified on the same day as Jesus. This thief ridiculed Jesus and Ed designed him sinking well below the cross member, signifying that he is just hanging meat.

45 "May Day Revelers: The Origins of the Maypole Dance," Historical Harmonies, accessed September 3, 2017, http://www.historicalharmonies.org/mapypoledanceorigins.htm.

46 "What is the MARK of CAIN?" The Bible Study Site, , accessed September 3, 2017, http://www.biblestudy.org/basicart/what-is-the-mark-of-cain.html.

The entire panel series is made of black walnut from around the world. Ed used black walnut to symbolize death and the darkness that descended on the scene as Christ died. Ed used full and half-cut pieces of diamond shaped black walnut to create the effect of darkness.

THE VEIL

This is the last panel series in the trilogy and it is named *The Veil*. Ed says this series represents death itself as he perceives it. Others may perceive it differently. Ed also reveals that he is in each one of these panels but assigned a different task in each.

The next changing of the times is coming, but only the Father knows when. No one can predict when it will be, but on that day, the Great Energy will fold this current reality up and this sphere will go back to its original position before the Garden of Eden. Ed claims that the only thing his studies concluded is that when we leave this sphere in death, we take what we have learned with us to the next sphere. We are on a continual educational trip.

According to Ed, the essence of your life never gets tired. It's the physical transport that gets tired—your legs, your fingers, your arms. But as you sleep, your mind doesn't sleep; it communicates with itself—the right and left side of the brain communicates with the soul. It communicates what it has learned and it makes a permanent record in the soul.

A. The center panel represents death. They are taking Jesus off the cross after hanging there for three to four hours. His body is loose, not stiff as dead bodies this old usually are. While Christ's body is surely dead, the normal processes associated with death are not taking place.

B. The person to the left of Jesus represents Ed. He is taking Jesus's arm and gently helping him down.

C. The person below Ed, at the bottom left of the center panel, is the accuser and he is pointing his finger at Ed, not Christ. He is accusing Ed of crucifying Christ.

D. The masked person to the right of Jesus is on a stepladder because Jesus is raised. The person below this man is unmasked and gently helping Christ off the cross.

E. At the bottom of the right panel is the name of the series, *The Veil*. In the Old Testament tabernacle, within the Holy of Holies, the sacred room where God dwelled was covered by a thick curtain known as the veil. This veil shielded God from sinful man. Only the high priests were allowed to enter once a year on the Day of Atonement, and were required to completely cleanse themselves before entering. When Jesus died on the cross, the veil was torn from top to bottom, allowing us access to God through Jesus's atonement for our sins. According to Ed, we are now in the presence of God, the very center of Jehovah and the Holy Spirit, by the product of their love, Jesus.

F. Above the name of the panel are three people praising and worshiping Jesus. Ed is the one hidden behind the person on the left.

G. Above them is an archangel sent from God to watch over those present and to offer comfort and understanding. This archangel is not there to see or experience death, but to serve God.

Ed created the archangel in absolute white with gold trim wearing a crown; one we will all receive. *"I have fought the good fight, I have finished the race, I have kept the faith. Now there is in store for me the crown of righteousness, which the Lord, the righteous Judge, will award to me on that day—and not only to me, but also to all who have longed for his appearing."* (2 Timothy 4:7-8).

H. At the far-left panel at the bottom is Ed's signature, 6-22-34, and the year Ed completed this panel: 2000.

I. There are four people looking on in amazement as Jesus is removed from the cross. Ed is the one on the far left hiding behind the others. He didn't want anyone to see him because he just crucified Jesus.

Above them are two angels who have not been crowned yet. One is crying because he thinks that time has now ceased with the death of Jesus. The other consoles him and explains that this is the way it has always been and that Jesus will live again. They cannot kill life or love, but can modify law. Ed believed that we are no longer under the law, but are under love.

Ed used blood wood to depict the name of the panel and in other areas as well. He claims this wood best symbolizes that Jesus's blood did not coagulate like normal blood does when the body dies.

THE BEST MAN

Ed named this panel *The Best Man*. He said he could have named it *"The Shaman"* or *"The Rabbi"* or *"The Priest"* because it is anyone who has earned the right, over a period of time and much study, to counsel the bride and groom on what to expect in marriage. Ed explains that every culture has its own best man; the one who has a right, because of age and education, to interpret what we see and feel.

At the time of Christ, the best man at a wedding, or as scripture calls, "friend of the bridegroom," had a specific job to do before the wedding took place. In Eastern culture, there were several stages to a wedding, including the arrangement, the dowry, the betrothal, the wedding ceremony and feast, and the consummation.[47]

Often, families arranged for the marriage of their sons and daughters before they were born. Once the bride and groom were agreed upon and the time for planning the wedding arrived, a friend of the bridegroom was selected to go to the home of the bride and discuss the character of the betrothed, as well as to negotiate the dowry (payment for the bride) and betrothal (engagement) contract.

The betrothal period could last a year or more and was considered sacred and binding. The bride would leave her home and go to the home of the groom where she was counseled and cared for by the mother of the bridegroom (or mother-in-law). The groom would give gifts to the family of the bride and may also perform work for the father of the bride during this period. The bride and groom could communicate with each other only through the friend of the groom.

After the wedding ceremony and feast, the bride and groom consummate their marriage. The friend of the bridegroom was expected to listen outside the door for the cheer of the groom, ensuring the bride remained pure during the betrothal period. Once he heard the cheer, the friend of the bridegroom would report back to

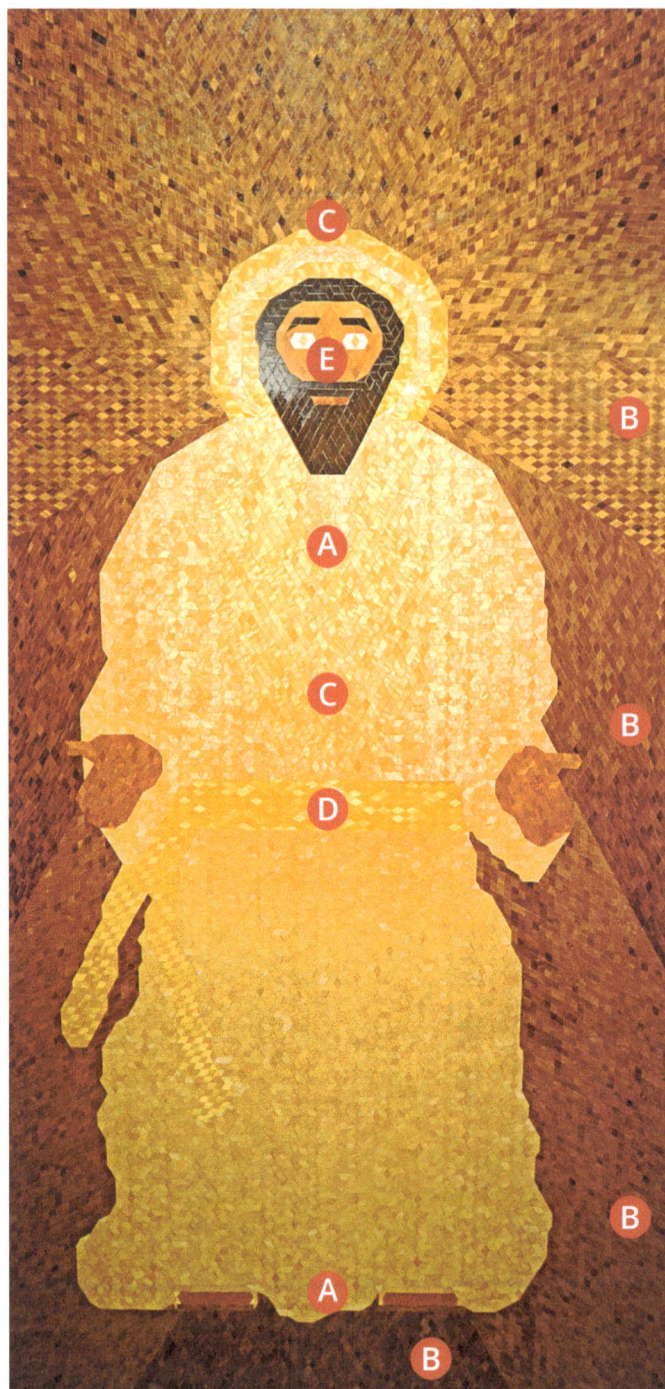

the family and friends that their marriage had been consummated.[48]

A. There are multiple meanings for the best man in this panel. The first is that this is Jesus Christ after the crucifixion and he is raised from the dead, as you can see from the holes in his hands, reminding us of his sacrifice for all of us. He is welcoming us back to him, though he has never left. Jesus is operating

47 Steve Santini, "Spiritual Representations of Divine Union in the Living Allegory of the Eastern Betrothal and Wedding Feast," Musterion8,com, October 1, 2013, accessed May 29, 2017, http://www.musterion8.com/wedding.html.

48 Steve Santini, "Spiritual Representations of Divine Union in the Living Allegory of the Eastern Betrothal and Wedding Feast," Musterion8,com, October 1, 2013, accessed May 29, 2017, http://www.musterion8.com/wedding.html.

in the spirit of holiness and he is teaching us how to reach the great banquet that they are preparing in heaven. His feet are not touching the ground symbolizing that he is risen.

A second interpretation is that this is the representation of the Holy Spirit today, getting us ready for the banquet that is yet to come. Revelations 19:9 says: *"Then the angel said to me, 'Write this: Blessed are those who are invited to the wedding supper of the Lamb!' And he added, 'These are the true words of God.'"* Jesus is the bridegroom, the church is the bride, and the friend of the bridegroom is the Holy Spirit. Ed, again, is explaining that the Holy Spirit is female, the mother of Christ, and mother to us all. We are depending on the Holy Spirit to get us ready for the wedding. Just as the mother-in-law prepared the bride to be married to the bridegroom, the Holy Spirit is preparing us. Jesus paid our dowry already and now we are in the betrothal period before the wedding. The Holy Spirit is preparing us, inviting the guests, and making all the arrangements.

B. Ed designed this panel with color variation from black to white, coming together as gray. In scripture, black symbolizes total ignorance and darkness; the further away you are from the Great Energy, the darker you will be. White represents total enlightenment; the closer you are to the Great Energy, the more knowledge you have. The many angles of the rays of light and variations in color represent the Holy Spirit teaching us as we come out of the darkness into the light. As Ed used various angles of light on this panel, so also does the Holy Spirit teach us about various angles of approach, stages of life and concepts about life to ponder.

C. The best man is dressed in a white gown and has a white aura around his head, symbolizing his complete enlightenment. Ed also perceives the aura as a totem; his totem, telling us the story of his humanity. He experienced beatings and rejection, but never perceived them as punishment. Jehovah did not come to punish us, but to teach us love.

D. The best man is wearing a gold sash to signify the truth about our relationship with God is all being held together with gold.

E. The eyes are green and will follow you around the room. Green surrounds the throne of God, His mind, and His absolute peace.

Ed used four kinds of wood throughout this panel. The two most prevalent are black walnut and cherry. Black walnut symbolizes darkness and cherry symbolizes whiteness and purity. The gold sash is a symbol of the softness of the Holy Spirit.

THE QUEST

Ed named this panel *The Quest* with the message that we are all on a quest to find the job that God created us to embrace. There is a great deal of symbolism in this panel, and like the other panels, there are multiple meanings.

Ed believed that the male is born with a heart of stone. He is the king of the world and everything is here because he is here. Man's main tenets are law, knowledge, and wisdom. As he grows a little older, around 12 to 15, he discovers a thing called the "soft spot" – it is love. Because it is not a principal trait of his, he is experiencing a new feeling. He starts to feel the love of his mother, or his sister, or the little girl down the street, and he realizes that the female heart is soft. The female's main tenents are faith, hope, and love. While the female does have law and the male has love, God created them purposefully with their primary traits and gave them the job and the ability to teach each other.

One symbolic meaning for this panel is that this is a portrait of Ed on his quest. He explains that this is his quest and no one else's. It is his way of thinking and may not be for everyone. This panel represents Ed's heart, and his job is to translate very ancient writings and concepts using symbols so that modern man can understand the difference between law and love. Ed learned that man believes in himself when it comes to law, knowledge, and wisdom, and he is doing his job; but eventually he needs to also experience love.

Ed knew that he was given a very specific job and that he was perfectly suited to complete his job. It is the only place from which he derived happiness, and it was his quest to investigate and explain to all of us the ancient symbols of law and love, of male and female. Using colors, configurations, and symbols, he tried to pass on the knowledge he gained to other people who need this information. Ed said his work was not a study in theology, but a study about the male and how the male was created unequal with a heart of stone, and needs the faith, hope, and love of the female—his mother, his sister, the little girl down the street—to turn his heart of

stone to a heart of love.

According to Ed, the male/female concept is law loving love, and love loving law. It is the male understanding the female perspective and her purpose, and the female understanding the male perspective and his purpose. Ed hoped this would cause us to really think of ourselves and understand ourselves, and then look at things from the other perspective. When the female looks at law from a man's perspective, she can understand that it is needed to govern and regulate us so that we don't hurt each other and just do whatever we want. The male looking at love from the female perspective understands that love for one another will stop us from hurting or killing each other. The same goes for faith and hope, knowledge and wisdom. It is the combination of these attributes together, and the male and female together, that gives us peace and allows us to govern ourselves. If we look at the parts of the body—the heart, the blood, the brain—they each have a job to do, but they need the other parts in order to do the job successfully or they'll all die.

A. Ed's self-portrait, he claims, is him after he dies.

B. In the bottom left corner is a very light cross, which Ed identified as his tombstone.

C. Ed, in this panel, has experienced the resurrection and has come back to do his same job only on a higher plane, which is symbolized as he is on a step above the tombstone. He is at the next stage of his existence and he is at the door calling people from all over, even other planets, to come to the Great Energy and bring their heart, like Ed has, so the Great Energy can mold it.

D. Ed is holding what may appear to be his own heart, but if you look at it differently, it may also be a door knocker, a heart on a pillow, or a crown. It could also represent multiple quests.

E. Inside the window is a faint outline of a face. Ed suggested this could be you inside as the Great Energy calls you, or it could be the Great Energy inside, faceless, as He hears you calling for him when you need Him, like when you are hurt and you say, "Oh God, please help me."

F. This was Ed's house as a child, and he says he was born into royalty; his father was king, his mother was queen, and he was the product of their love for each other. The purple color of the roof illustrates the royalty of his family.

G. The hinges on the door are an illusion. They are on the wrong side of the door, they are three different sizes, and they are not connected so the door cannot open. They have no value.

H. The doves above the door represent Ed's mother and father, and the male and female relationship. Ed's mother is in the nest and Ed's father is coming to feed her with a worm in his mouth, and she can then feed Ed, their son. God the father is coming to feed his wife, the Holy Spirit, who then nourishes their son, Jesus. Ed also says the male dove is holding a mistletoe, representing Ed's Scandinavian heritage where kissing under the mistletoe originated.

I. The name of the panel, *The Quest,* is written in a scroll at the bottom of the panel.

J. Ed's signature, 6-22-34, is also there on the bottom right, and below the signature is 1989, the year Ed made this panel.

Another legitimate interpretation of the panel is that this is Christ knocking on your door. As it says in Revelations 3:20: *"Behold, I stand at the door, and knock: if any man hear my voice, and open the door, I will come in to him, and will sup with him, and he with me."*

The various colors throughout the panel have special meaning. Ed says each color has its own concept or knowledge within scripture in the Old Testament. There are color harmonies, like the rainbow with its perfect harmony and its protective arch over us.

Purple means royalty—Ed's mother and father were king and queen; Christ is King.

Green is the color of peace—it is the center of the rainbow, the leaves on the tree, and the center of Ed's father's home with quiet love and no shouting or blaming.

White is purity in scripture and purity in thought. It isn't about what someone wears, but what is inside him or her, the real spirit. There are men with absolutely pure hearts, which is where sainthood comes in. We are all born with pure hearts, and everything else we've been given is learned from either the male or female.

The panel is constructed of oak and mahogany. Oak is strong and hard, representing the male. It is used in the stones of the house. Mahogany is soft and represents the female. It is used to make the heart.

Ed believed he was given the job of creating this panel. He started off suffering through the same argument of self-pity, telling himself he couldn't possibly do it and it was beyond his comprehension. When he got through feeling sorry for himself, the Father said, "Ok let's get to work." He gave Ed the ideas and used Ed's hands to accomplish them. Ed claimed he was allowed to see, but that he was merely the hands of God's illustration. We have not seen the sum of what God has created us for or what God has created for us.

Ed says the panels were created for you. Everything that he went through to design and build them was done for you so that you can possibly understand what your quest in life is. He said, "You get to the point where you need to understand the soft spot, and that is love in your heart, and love for others no matter how they treat you."

CONCLUSION

Ed Lantzer's mosaic panels depicting biblical accounts of creation and the birth, life, and crucifixion of Jesus Christ continue to amaze visitors wherever they are on display. They have traveled from Michigan to Indiana and to Illinois to inspire and astound those who come to witness them. One major challenge that the My Father's Love Foundation board regularly faces is finding adequate venues to exhibit them.

When they are not on display, all thirty enormous works of art are carefully loaded up and put away until another suitable location is found for them to come out and inspire once again. While numerous organizations and corporations have reached out to MFLF, offering space to exhibit them, many do not meet the strict criteria required. One necessity is that the space be large enough to get the panels through the door, set them up, and house them with enough room for the public to come in and view them. Another condition, and Ed's most notable one, is that they be absolutely free for everyone to see. The possibility for an organization to financially profit from them in any way is explicitly forbidden.

The ultimate goal of the MFLF board is to find a permanent home for the panels so they never have to be taken down and stored away from the public eyes they were built to be viewed through. Until that day comes, the panels often find themselves homeless, just like Ed.

To learn more about My Father's Love Foundation and how you can contribute to their mission of getting Ed's panels and their inspiring story out to the public, visit www.myfatherslove.info.

Now that you've read about the panels and consider Ed's meanings behind the symbolism throughout, do you have other possible meanings or ideas? Email info@myfatherslove.info to share your thoughts. While Ed offered his intentions for the designs and symbols, he always left it open to the viewer by saying, "You decide."

AdamEve - Panel 1

AdamEve - Panel 2

Moses and the Ten Commandments

My Mother's Love - Panel 1

My Mother's Love - Panel 2

My Mother's Love - Panel 3

My Mother's Love - Panel 4

My Mother's Love - Panel 5

My Mother's Love - Panel 6

My Mother's Love - Panel 7

My Father's Love - Panel 1

My Father's Love - Panel 2

My Father's Love - Panel 3

My Father's Love - Panel 4

My Father's Love - Panel 5

My Father's Love - Panel 6

My Father's Love - Panel 7

Simon and The Lamb - Panel 1

Simon and The Lamb - Panel 2

Raising of Christ - Panel 1

Raising of Christ - Panel 2

Raising of Christ - Panel 3

Daddy - Panel 1

Daddy - Panel 2

Daddy - Panel 3

The Veil - Panel 1

The Veil - Panel 2

The Veil - Panel 3

The Best Man

The Quest

BIBLIOGRAPHY

"Bee." Symbols. October 14, 2015. Accessed January 5, 2017. http://symbols.ehibou.com/bee/.

Benner, Jeff A. "The Ancient Hebrew Alphabet - Shin." Ancient-Hebrew.org. Accessed January 11, 2017. http://www.ancient-hebrew.org/alphabet_letters_shin.html.

Bullinger, E. W. "The Spiritual Significance of Numbers." TheRain.org. Accessed October 7, 2017. http://www.therain.org/appendixes/app10.html.

Caldwell, Chris K. "Why is the number one not prime?" The Prime Pages. Accessed February 8, 2017. https://primes.utm.edu/notes/faq/one.html.

Calter, Paul. Squaring the Circle: Geometry in Art and Architecture. John Wiley, 2008. 1998. Accessed January 20, 2018. https://www.dartmouth.edu/~matc/math5.geometry/unit3/unit3.html.

"Chi Rho." ReligionFacts. October 29, 2016. Accessed October 14, 2017. http://www.religionfacts.com/chi-rho.

"Christogram." New World Encyclopedia. Accessed January 12, 2017. http://www.newworldencyclopedia.org/p/index.php?title=Christogram&oldid=969357.

"Cross of Tau." Symbols.com. Accessed March 31, 2017. http://www.symbols.com/symbol/cross-of-tau.

"Elijah." A Virtual Passover - Elijah. Accessed January 5, 2017. http://avirtualpassover.com/elijah.htm.

"Elijah, Chair of." Jewish Virtual Library. Accessed January 7, 2017. http://www.jewishvirtuallibrary.org/elijah-chair-of.

Grebenc, Richard J. "Carrying the Cross with Simon of Cyrene." Homiletic & Pastoral Review. April 13, 2014. Accessed July 9, 2017. http://www.hprweb.com/2014/04/carrying-the-cross-with-simon-of-cyrene/.

Gyurme, Tenzin. Sacred Numerology of ThoTh. LULU COM, 2015. Accessed January 21, 2018. https://books.google.com/books?id=K1tRAgAAQBAJ&pg=PA48&dq=The Sacred Numerology of ThoTh four stars&hl=en&sa=X&ved=0ahUKEwio1bKYqejYAhVW3m MKHa1TDmkQ6AEIKTAA#v=onepage&q&f=false.

Hall, Manly P. "Pythagorean Mathematics." Secret Teachings of All Ages: Pythagorean Mathematics. Accessed February 8, 2017. http://www.sacred-texts.com/eso/sta/sta16.htm.

"John 1:1 Greek Text Analysis." BibleHub. Accessed January 10, 2017. http://biblehub.com/text/john/1-1.htm.

"John 4:42 Greek Text Analysis." BibleHub. Accessed December 29, 2016. http://biblehub.com/text/john/4-42.htm.

Kalvesmaki, Joel. "Generating the World of Numbers: Pythagorean and Platonist Number Symbolism in the First Century." Generating the World of Numbers: Pythagorean and Platonist Number Symbolism in the First Century. Accessed February 07, 2017. https://chs.harvard.edu/CHS/article/display/6304.

"Loaded Dice." Wordnik.com. Accessed September 3, 2017. https://www.wordnik.com/words/loaded%20dice.

"Luca 23 - Nouă Traducere În Limba Română (NTLR)." Biblica. Accessed January 4, 2017. https://www.biblica.com/bible/ntlr/luca/23/.

"Luke 23 - New Living Translation (NLT)." Biblica. Accessed January 4, 2017. https://www.biblica.com/bible/nlt/luke/23/.

MacArthur, John. "Who Were the Wise Men?" Grace to You. February 05, 1978. Accessed February 8, 2017.   https://www.gty.org/library/sermons-library/2182/who-were-the-wise-men.

"May Day Revelers: The Origins of the Maypole Dance." Historical Harmonies. Accessed September 3, 2017. http://www.historicalharmonies.org/mapypoledanceorigins.htm.

McClister, David . "The Scourging of Jesus." Truth Magazine Online - Conservative Christian Bible Study Materials. Accessed July 16, 2017. http://www.truthmagazine.com/archives/volume44/v440106010.htm.

"Meaning of Numbers in the Bible: The Number 6." BibleStudy.org. Accessed December 29, 2016. http://www.biblestudy.org/bibleref/meaning-of-numbers-in-bible/6.html.

"Meaning of Numbers in the Bible: The Number 7." BibleStudy.org. Accessed December 29, 2016. http://www.biblestudy.org/bibleref/meaning-of-numbers-in-bible/7.html.

Oord, Thomas Jay. "Agape Theology." For The Love of Wisdom and The Wisdom of Love. December 28, 2016. Accessed October 13, 2016. http://thomasjayoord.com/index.php/blog/archives/agape_theology.

"Ouroboros: Symbolic representation of coming full circle (cycle)." Ouroboros - Crystalinks. Accessed March 31, 2017. http://www.crystalinks.com/ouroboros.html.

"Rachel: The Woman in Whom Romance and Tragedy Were Blended." All the Women of the Bible - Rachel. Accessed September 04, 2017. https://www.Biblegateway.com/resources/all-women-Bible/Rachel.

"Roman Standard." Tribunes and Triumphs. Accessed January 10, 2017. http://www.tribunesandtriumphs.org/roman-army/roman-standard.htm.

Santini, Steve . "Spiritual Representations of Divine Union in the Living Allegory of the Eastern Betrothal and Wedding Feast." Musterion8,com. October 1, 2013. Accessed May 29, 2017. http://www.musterion8.com/wedding.html.

"Savior." Google Translate. Accessed December 29, 2016. https://translate.google.com/?um=1&ie=UTF-8&hl=en&client=tw-ob#en/el/Savior.

"Six-Point Star (Hexagram; Star of David)." ReligionFacts. January 19, 2017. Accessed January 12, 2017. http://www.religionfacts.com/six-point-star.

"Snake Eyes." Wolfram MathWorld. Accessed September 3, 2017. http://mathworld.wolfram.com/SnakeEyes.html.

"The Birth of Jesus." Luke 2 - Bible Gateway. Accessed March 5, 2017. https://www.biblegateway.com/passage/?search=Luke%2B2.

"The Hebrew Names for God - El." Hebrew for Christians. Accessed July 8, 2017. http://www.hebrew4christians.com/Names_of_G-d/El/el.html.

"The Lady of the Lake." Britannia.com. Accessed October 18, 2017. http://www.britannia.com/history/biographies/nimue.html.

"The Meaning of Aura Colors." Chakra Anatomy. Accessed January 9, 2017. http://www.chakra-anatomy.com/aura-colors.html.

"The Triangle." The State of Symbols. Accessed January 12, 2017. http://thestateofsymbols.com/the-triangle/.

Theodorou, Linda. "T is for Tamata." Churches in Greece. January 01, 1970. Accessed January 12, 2017. http://churchesingreece.blogspot.com/2014/01/t-is-for-tamata.html.

Van Biema, David. "How readers 'solved' the mystery of the prayer wheel." Religion News Service. July 07, 2016. Accessed January 10, 2017. http://religionnews.com/2015/05/15/readers-solved-mystery-prayer-wheel/.

"What is the MARK of CAIN?" The Bible Study Site. Accessed September 3, 2017. http://www.biblestudy.org/basicart/what-is-the-mark-of-cain.html.

"Who were the 12 disciples?" Bibleinfo.com. Accessed January 6, 2017. http://www.biblein fo.com/en/questions/who-were-twelve-disciples#simon-zealot.

"Who were the 12 disciples?" Bibleinfo.com. Accessed January 6, 2017. http://www.biblein fo.com/en/questions/who-were-twelve-disciples#jude-thaddeus.

"Who were the 12 disciples?" Bibleinfo.com. Accessed January 6, 2017. http://www.biblein fo.com/en/questions/who-were-twelve-disciples#matthew-levi.

"Why Did the Magi Bring Gold, Frankincense and Myrrh?" Biblical Archaeology Society. Accessed March 05, 2017. https://www.biblicalarchaeology.org/daily/people-cultures-in-the-bible/jesus-historical-jesus/why-did-the-magi-bring-gold-frankincense-and-myrrh/.

Wood, Larry. "Lunar Eclipse." Bible Doctrine News. Accessed January 12, 2017. http://www.biblenews1.com/history0/20000120eclipse.htm.

"לש [SHEL] – Who Does this belong to?" My Hebrew Word מילה בעברית. April 27, 2014. Accessed January 11, 2017. https://myhebrewwords.wordpress.com/2014/04/27/5-%D7%A9%D7%9C-shel-who-does-this-belong-to/.

www.ingramcontent.com/pod-product-compliance
Lightning Source LLC
Chambersburg PA
CBHW061136030426

42334CB00003B/59